The Public
Speaking Guide

The Public Speaking Guide

Joseph A. DeVito

Hunter College of the City University of New York

■ HarperCollins*CollegePublishers*

Acquisitions Editor: Daniel F. Pipp
Project Editor: Thomas R. Farrell
Design Supervisor and Cover Design: Wendy A. Fredericks
Production Manager: Willie Lane
Compositor: Black Dot, Inc.
Printer, Binder, and Cover Printer: Malloy Lithographing, Inc.

The Public Speaking Guide

Library of Congress Cataloging-in-Publication Data

DeVito, Joseph A., (date)–
    The public speaking guide / Joseph A. DeVito.
        p.   cm.
    Includes Bibliographical references (p.).
    ISBN 0-06-501292-5
    1. Public speaking.   I. Title.
PN4121.D3893   1994
808.5'1--dc20   93-46259
                                              CIP

97 9 8 7 6

CONTENTS

Preface   vii

CHAPTER 1   INTRODUCTION TO PUBLIC SPEAKING   1

CHAPTER 2   SELECTING YOUR TOPIC AND PURPOSE   8

CHAPTER 3   ANALYZING YOUR AUDIENCE   17

CHAPTER 4   RESEARCHING YOUR SPEECH   28

CHAPTER 5   DEVELOPING YOUR THESIS AND MAJOR PROPOSITIONS
             36

CHAPTER 6   USING SUPPORTING MATERIALS   42

CHAPTER 7   ORGANIZING YOUR SPEECH   56

CHAPTER 8   WORDING YOUR SPEECH   71

CHAPTER 9   DEVELOPING INTRODUCTIONS, CONCLUSIONS, AND
             TRANSITIONS   80

CHAPTER 10   PERFECTING DELIVERY   91

CHAPTER 11   THE INFORMATIVE SPEECH   99

CHAPTER 12   THE PERSUASIVE SPEECH   107

             POSTSCRIPT   114

Bibliography   115

PREFACE

Courses in human communication vary widely in their coverage of public speaking. Some devote little attention to it because of their focus on theory rather than skills and also because public speaking is covered in depth in other courses. Other human communication courses devote up to 70 percent of their time to public speaking and focus on both theory and skills. To respond to these important differences, without slighting either theory or skills, the public speaking units in the sixth edition of *Human Communication* were recast to focus largely on the theoretical aspects: the nature of public speaking, the standards of criticism, the principles for communicating information and for persuading, and the dimensions of logical, emotional, and credibility appeals. The topics are those that anyone who aims to understand human communication needs to know.

These discussions also serve as a solid foundation for the more practical instruction that appears in this book. *The Public Speaking Guide* is designed for those students who want to learn not only the theory but also how to prepare and deliver a public speech. It is devoted entirely to the skills of public speaking; it provides the practical, how-to-do-it advice needed to prepare and present an effective informative or persuasive speech.

USING THE PUBLIC SPEAKING GUIDE

This guide is a supplement to and an expansion of the three units (Units 19, 20, and 21) in *Human Communication* devoted to public speaking. Therefore, read those three units first; they will provide you with a broad foundation in the definition, theory, and principles of public speaking. Once you understand the basic structure and function of public speaking, you will find the practical advice more logical and easier to apply.

After you have read the three units in *Human Communication,* begin reading the chapters in this book. The chapters follow the process of preparing a speech, so work on your speech as you read this book. For example, select your topic and purpose immediately after reading Chapter 2 ("Selecting Your Topic and Purpose"). Analyze and consider potential adaptions to your specific audience immediately after reading Chapter 3 ("Analyzing Your Audience").

When working on an informative speech, read Chapter 11 ("The Informative Speech"), and when working on a persuasive speech, read Chapter 12 ("The Persuasive Speech") early in your preparation.

JOSEPH A. DEVITO

CHAPTER **1**

INTRODUCTION TO PUBLIC SPEAKING

CHAPTER CONTENTS

The Benefits of Public Speaking
    Enhance Academic and Career Skills
    Refine General Communication Abilities
    Increase Public Speaking Abilities

Preparing and Delivering a Public Speech

Public Speaking Criticism
    Say Something Positive
    Be Specific
    Be Objective
    Be Constructive
    Focus on Behavior
    Own Your Own Criticism
    Remember the Irreversibility of Communication
    Guidelines for Speech Criticism

CHAPTER GOALS

After completing this chapter, you should be able to

1. identify the benefits to be derived from studying public speaking

2. identify the nine steps in preparing a public speech

3. explain the principles to follow and the questions to ask in constructively criticizing a speech

This introductory chapter explains the benefits you should derive from the study of public speaking, the steps in preparing an effective speech, and how criticism might be used to help you improve your public speaking abilities.

THE BENEFITS OF PUBLIC SPEAKING

Why should you study public speaking? What benefits will you derive from the time and effort you will invest? What are the payoffs you can expect from your investment? Here we discuss a few of the more important ones.

Enhance Academic and Career Skills

As you learn public speaking, you also will learn a wide variety of other skills that will help you throughout your college and professional careers. A few additional abilities that you should refine in this course and that will help you throughout your career include how to

- explain complex concepts clearly
- research a wide variety of issues
- support an argument with all the available means of persuasion
- understand human motivation and be able to use your insights in persuasive encounters
- present yourself to others with confidence and self-assurance

Refine General Communication Abilities

Public speaking also will develop and refine your general communication abilities by helping you to improve competencies such as

- developing a more effective communication style
- enhancing your self-concept and self-esteem
- adjusting messages to specific listeners
- detecting and responding to feedback
- developing logical and emotional appeals
- developing and communicating your credibility
- increasing your ability to express constructive criticism
- improving listening skills
- organizing extended messages for clarity and persuasiveness
- refining your delivery skills

Increase Public Speaking Abilities

Speakers are not born; they are made. You become the speaker you are through instruction, exposure to different speeches, feedback, and your own learning experiences. Regardless of your present level of competence, you can improve through proper training—hence this course and this booklet.

At the end of this booklet and this course you should be a more competent, confident, and effective public speaker. You also should emerge a more competent and discerning critic of public communication.

The more comfortable you are as a public speaker, the more willing you will be to speak out. You will be more willing to support what you feel you should support and to protest what you feel you should protest. The study of public speaking is an essential part of any student's development into a more effective individual and social leader.

PREPARING AND DELIVERING A PUBLIC SPEECH

You're going to give a speech and you're anxious and unsure of what to say. What do you do? What do you speak about? How do you decide what to include in the speech? How should a speech be organized? At this point you probably have a lot more questions than answers, but that is the way it should be. By following the steps explained in this pamphlet, you will be able to prepare and present effective informative and persuasive speeches.

In this booklet we identify nine steps for preparing and presenting an effective speech. Although these nine steps (Figure 1.1) are presented in linear fashion (one after the other), the process of constructing a public speech seldom follows such a neat, logical sequence. You will probably not progress simply from Step 1, to 2, to 3, and so on. Instead, your progression might go more like this: Step 1, to Step 2, back again to Step 1, to Step 3, back again to Step 2, and so on throughout the preparation of your speech. For example, after selecting your subject and purpose (Step 1), you may progress to Step 2 and analyze your audience. On the basis of this analysis, however, you may wish to go back and modify your subject, your purpose, or both. Or, after you research the topic (Step 3), you may want more information on your audience and thus backtrack to Step 2.

For some speeches you may wish to focus first on your audience, asking yourself, What do these students want or need to know? What are they interested in? In other cases you may wish to examine your own feelings about what is especially important. For example, you may feel strongly about recycling, amnesty, gay-lesbian rights, or abortion, and you may feel it is important to instruct or convince others regarding these issues. Here you would begin with your own convictions and ask how you might adapt or relate this topic to your specific audience.

All this back and forth should not throw you off track. This is the way most people prepare speeches and written communications. So, although we present the steps in the order a speaker normally follows, remember that you are in charge of the process. Use the order of these steps as a guideline but break the sequence as you need to. As long as you cover all nine steps thoroughly, you should accomplish your goal.

9. Rehearse delivery
8. Construct conclusion, introduction, and transitions
7. Word the speech
6. Organize the speech materials
5. Support the major propositions
4. Formulate the thesis and major propositions
3. Research the topic
2. Analyze the audience
1. Select subject and purpose

FIGURE 1.1 The steps in preparing a public speech.

PUBLIC SPEAKING CRITICISM

In learning the art of public speaking, you will gain much insight from others' criticism of you as well as from your criticism of others. Here are some suggestions for making criticism easier and more constructive.

Say Something Positive

Part of your function as a critic is to strengthen the already positive aspects of someone's public speaking performance. There are always positive characteristics, and it is more productive to concentrate on these first.

Be Specific

In commenting on supporting materials, for example, tell the speaker why they were effective or ineffective. Were they realistic? Were they convincing? Were they presented effectively? In all cases, specify—to the extent you can—positive alternatives. Here is an example:

> I thought the way in which you introduced your statistics was vague. I wasn't sure where the statistics came from or how recent or reliable they were. It might have been better to say something like "The 1990 U.S. Census figures show that. . . ." In this way we would know that the statistics were recent and the most reliable available.

Be Objective

In criticizing a speech, transcend your own biases and see the speech as objectively as possible. Take special care not to evaluate a speech positively *because* it presents a position with which you agree or negatively *because* it presents a position with which you disagree.

Be Constructive

Give the speaker the insight you feel will prove useful in future public speaking transactions. To say "The introduction didn't gain my attention" doesn't tell the speaker how he or she might have gained your attention. Instead, you might say "The example about the computer crash would have more effectively gained my attention in the introduction."

Focus on Behavior

Focus criticism on what the speaker said and did during the actual speech. Try not to mindread, to assume that you know why the speaker did one thing rather than another. Instead of stating *why* you think the speaker did what he or she did, state *what* the speaker did and what you think the speaker should have done differently.

Own Your Own Criticism

Take responsibility for your criticism. The best way to express this ownership is to use "I-messages" rather than "you-messages." Instead of saying "You needed better research," say, "I would have been more persuaded if you used more recent research." Also, avoid attributing what you found wrong to others. Instead of saying "Nobody was able to understand you," say, "*I* had difficulty understanding you. It would have helped *me* if you had spoken more slowly."

Remember the Irreversibility of Communication

Communication is irreversible. Once something is said, it cannot be unsaid. Remember this when offering criticism, especially criticism that may be too negative. If in doubt, err on the side of gentleness.

Guidelines for Speech Criticism

The following questions are in the nature of a beginner's guide to speech criticism. These questions come from the topics listed in Figure 1.1, which we cover in the remaining chapters. But they don't cover all possible issues. View these questions as a guide to *some* of the issues to look for. You will also find it helpful to use these questions as a checklist for your own speeches. A sample critique form that covers these same issues is presented in Figure 1.2.

The Subject and Purpose   The speech subject should be worthwhile, relevant, and interesting to the audience. The speech purpose should be clear and sufficiently narrow so that it can be achieved in the allotted time.

1. Is the subject a worthwhile one?
2. Is the subject relevant and interesting to the audience and to the speaker?
3. Is the information presented of benefit to the audience in some way?
4. What is the general purpose of the speech (to inform, to persuade)? Is this clear to the audience?
5. Is the specific topic sufficiently narrow?

The Audience, Occasion, and Context   A public speech is designed for a specific audience and occasion and takes into account the characteristics of the audience.

6. Has the speaker taken into consideration the age; sex; cultural factors; occupation, income, and status; and religion and religiousness of the audience?
7. Is the speech adapted to the occasion and context?

Research   A public speech needs to be based on accurate and reliable information. The topic needs to be thoroughly researched and the speaker needs to demonstrate a command of the subject matter.

8. Is the speech adequately researched? Do the sources appear reliable and up to date?
9. Does the speaker have a thorough understanding of the subject?
10. Is the speaker's competence communicated to the audience?

The Thesis and Major Propositions   The public speech should have one clear thesis to which the major propositions in the speech are clearly related.

11. Is the thesis clear and limited to one idea?
12. Are the main propositions clearly related to the thesis?

Supporting Materials   The speech's propositions must be supported by a variety of appropriate supporting materials that explain them or establish their validity.

Public Speaking Critique Form

Evaluation key: 1 = excellent; 2 = good; 3 = fair; 4 = needs improvement; 5 = needs lots of improvement. *Circle or underscore* items that the speaker needs to *work on;* write in additional items requiring attention.

Speaker _____ . Date _____ .

Speech _____ .

_____ **Subject and Purpose**

Work on: selecting more worthwhile subject; making subject relevant and interesting to audience; clarifying purpose; narrowing purpose

_____ **Audience, Occasion, Context**

Work on: relating topic and supporting materials to specific audience, occasion, and context

_____ **Research**

Work on: doing more extensive research; using more reliable sources; stressing your command of the subject

_____ **Thesis and Major Propositions**

Work on: clarifying thesis; limiting thesis to one central idea; relating propositions to thesis

_____ **Supporting Materials**

Work on: using more support; using more varied and appropriate support; relating support more directly to the propositions

_____ **Organization**

Work on: using a clear thought pattern; making pattern clear to audience

_____ **Style and Language**

Work on: clarity, vividness, appropriateness, personal style, forcefulness/power; sentence structure

_____ **Conclusion, Introduction, Transitions**

Work on: conclusions' summary, motivation, closure; introduction's attention, S-A-T connection, orientation; using more transitions

_____ **Delivery**

Work on: eye contact, eliminating distracting mannerisms, gestures, volume, rate

_____ **General Evaluation**

FIGURE 1.2

13. Is each major proposition adequately supported? Are the supporting materials varied and appropriate to the speech and to the propositions?
14. Do the supporting materials amplify what they purport to amplify? Do they prove what they purport to prove?
15. Are the evidence and argument, motivational appeals, and credibility appeals convincing?

Organization   The speech materials should be organized into a meaningful whole to facilitate the audience's understanding.

16. Is the body of the speech organized in a pattern that is appropriate to the speech topic? To the audience?
17. Is the pattern of organization clear to the audience? Does it help the audience follow the speech?

Style and Language   The language and style of the speech should help the audience understand the speaker's message. It should be consistent in tone with the speech topic and purpose.

18. Does the language help the audience to understand what the speaker is saying? Is an oral rather than a written style used?
19. Is the language clear, vivid, appropriate, personal, and forceful? Are the sentences generally short, direct, active, and positive?

The Conclusion, Introduction, and Transitions   The conclusion should summarize the major points, motivate, and provide clear and crisp closure. The introduction should gain attention, establish a connection among speaker, audience, and topic, and orient the audience. Transitions should connect the various parts of the speech and provide guideposts for the audience to help them follow the speaker's train of thought.

20. Does the conclusion effectively summarize the main points identified in the speech, motivate the audience, and wrap up the speech, providing recognizable closure?
21. Does the introduction gain attention, establish a relationship among speaker, audience, and topic, and provide a clear orientation to the subject matter of the speech?
22. Are there adequate transitions? Do the transitions help the audience to better understand the development of the speech?

Delivery   Effective delivery should help maintain audience attention and reinforce the ideas in the speech.

23. Is extemporaneous delivery used? Is it used effectively?
24. Is the voice effective? Are volume, rate, articulation and pronunciation, and pauses used effectively?
25. Is the bodily action effective? Are eye contact, facial expression, posture, gestures, and gross bodily movement used to reinforce the message?

CHAPTER 2

SELECTING YOUR TOPIC AND PURPOSE

CHAPTER CONTENTS

Selecting a Topic
   What Is a Suitable Speech Topic?
   Finding Topics
Establishing Your Purpose
   General Purposes
   Specific Purposes

CHAPTER GOALS

After completing this chapter, you should be able to

1. identify the qualities of a suitable speech topic
2. limit a speech topic to manageable proportions
3. use a variety of methods to locate speech topics
4. phrase effective specific speech purposes

In this chapter we explain how you can find a suitable topic and how to establish the general and specific purposes of your speech.

SELECTING A TOPIC

Perhaps the question you are most concerned with is, "What will I talk about?" The answer, of course, depends on the situation you are in. And there will be many such occasions throughout your academic and professional life. For example, as a parent speaking to the PTA you might speak on admission standards, testing, or teacher-student relationships. As a member of a union called upon to react to the proposed contract, you might speak about wages, fringe benefits, or dues. As a member of a team working with a youth group, you might speak on new group activities, athletic plans, or safe sex practices. As a manager in an office, you might speak on the new computers, the plans for a day care center, or ways to evaluate new employees.

For your classroom speeches—where the objective is to learn the skills of public speaking—there are hundreds of things to talk about. Throughout this chapter we offer lots of suggestions for suitable speech topics. But before identifying specific suggestions we need to distinguish topics that are suitable from topics that are not.

What Is a Suitable Speech Topic?

A suitable speech topic should (1) be worthwhile and deal with matters of substance; (2) be appropriate to the speaker, audience, and occasion; and (3) be limited in scope.

Worthwhile The topics for a speech in a public speaking class should be *worthwhile*. Topics that are worthwhile have consequences that are significant for your listeners. The consequences may be educational, social, religious, political, economic, relational, or medical—to cite just a few examples—but they must be significant. In short, the topic must be important enough to merit the time and attention of a group of intelligent and educated persons.

Appropriate To be suitable a speech must be *appropriate* to you as the speaker, to the audience you will address, and to the occasion.

Appropriateness to the speaker is always difficult to determine, largely because it is difficult to see yourself from the point of view of the audience. Don't select a topic merely because it will fulfill the requirements of an assignment. Instead, select a topic about which you know something and would like to learn more. You will not only acquire new knowledge but also will discover the sources that will teach you more about the topic—for example, the major books, the relevant journals, and the noted authorities. Also, your own interest and enthusiasm will show during the speech; this, in turn, will help maintain the attention of your listeners and help establish your own credibility.

Look also at your topic in terms of its *appropriateness to the audience*. What are they interested in? What would they like to learn more about? Will they want to invest their time in listening to a speech about your topic? It is much easier to please an audience when you speak on a topic that interests them. Speaking in a class situation makes this potentially difficult decision a lot easier, since you can assume that your classmates are interested in many of the same things you are.

Your topic should also be *appropriate to the occasion*. For example, time limitations will exclude certain topics because they are too complex. You could not explain the problems with our educational system or propose a solution to the drug problem in a five-minute speech. While a classroom situation will probably offer few difficulties created by the "occasion," outside the classroom the occasion imposes a number of serious restrictions. Some occasions call for humorous subjects that would be out of place in other contexts. Speeches of personal experience may be appropriate in one context but inappropriate in another.

Limited in Scope   A suitable topic for a public speech is limited in scope. Probably the major problem for beginning speakers is that they attempt to cover a huge topic in too short a time; crime in the United States, why our tax structure should be changed, the sociology of film, and the like are too broad and try to cover too much. The inevitable result is that nothing specific is covered—everything is touched on but only on the surface. Invariably your listeners will go away with the feeling that they have gained nothing as a result of listening to your speech.

The process of narrowing and limiting your topic is simple and consists of repeatedly dividing the topic into its significant parts. Once you divide your general topic into its component parts, take one of these parts and divide it into its component parts. Continue with this process until the topic seems manageable, one that you can reasonably cover in some depth in the allotted time.

For example, take the topic of *television programs* as the first general topic area. You might divide this topic into such subtopics as *comedies, children's programs, educational programs, news shows, movies, soap operas, game shows,* and *sports programs*. Then take one of these topics—say, *comedies*—and divide it into subtopics. Perhaps you might consider it on a time basis and divide television comedy into its significant time periods: *pre-1960, 1961–1979, 1980 to the present*. Or, you might focus on *situation comedies*. Here you might examine a topic such as *women in television comedy, race relations in situation comedy,* or *family relationships in television comedies*. The resultant topic is at least beginning to look manageable. *Television programs,* without some limitation, would take a lifetime to cover adequately.

Construction of tree diagrams (where subtopics emerge like branches from a trunk) might clarify the process of narrowing a topic. Let us say, for example, that you want to do a speech on mass communication. You might develop a tree diagram with branches for the division that interests you most, as shown in Figure 2.1. Thus you can divide *mass communication* into *film, television, radio, newspapers,* and *magazines*. If *television* interests you most, then develop branches from *television. Comedy, news, soaps, sports,* and *game shows* would be appropriate. Now, suppose *soaps* most interest you. In this case you would create branches from *soaps,* perhaps *prime time* and *daytime*. Keep dividing the topic until you get a topic that is significant, appropriate to you and your audience, and manageable in the allotted time.

Finding Topics

Finding topics for speaking is a relatively easy process. Four ways to find topics are through surveys, news items, brainstorming, and the idea generator.

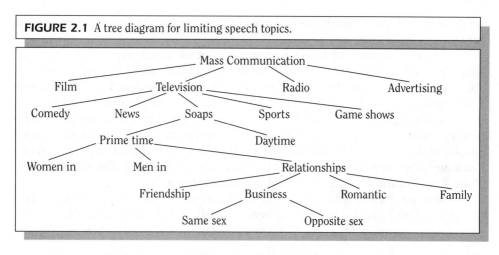

FIGURE 2.1 A tree diagram for limiting speech topics.

Surveys Look at some of the national and regional polls concerning what people think is important—the significant issues, the urgent problems. For example, a survey conducted by the Roper organization for H&R Block in *The American Public and the Income Tax System* (1978) found that Americans felt the most significant issues include lowering the crime rate, making the tax system fair, improving the educational system, improving the nation's defense capabilities, setting up a program to provide national health insurance for everyone, lowering unemployment, improving and protecting the environment, lowering Social Security taxes, and improving public transportation.

In a survey conducted by Public Research, respondents said they were concerned with these major problems confronting our country: crime and lawlessness, the tax burden of the working American, the rising costs of hospital and health care, unemployment, energy, the condition of older people, the declining quality of education, pollution of air and water, and the condition of minority members of our society.

In a survey conducted for *Psychology Today* (September 1981), the personal hopes and fears of Americans were investigated. Respondents named the following hopes: better or decent standard of living, good health for self, economic stability in general (no inflation), happy family life, peace of mind, emotional maturity, own a house or live in a better one, peace in the world, aspirations for children, good job (congenial work), wealth, employment, good health for family, and to be a normal, decent person. The greatest personal fears were lowered standard of living, ill health for self, war, economic instability in general, inflation, unemployment, ill health of family, and crime.

News Items Another useful starting point is a good newspaper or magazine. Here you will find important international and domestic issues, financial issues, and social issues all conveniently packaged in one place. The editorial page and the letters to the editor are also useful in learning what people are concerned about.

News magazines like *Time* and *Newsweek* and such financial magazines as *Forbes, Money,* and *Fortune* will provide a wealth of suggestions. Similarly, television news shows like *20/20, 60 Minutes, Firing Line,* and even the ubiquitous talk shows often identify the very issues that people are concerned with and consider controversial.

Brainstorming Another useful method is to brainstorm (Beebe & Masterson, 1990; Osborn, 1957). *Brainstorming,* a technique for bombarding a problem and generating as many ideas as possible, is explained in depth in *Human Communication* (Unit 16).

To use brainstorming to generate suitable speech topics, you would begin with your "problem," which in this case is "What will I talk about?" Then record any idea that occurs to you, using the four rules of brainstorming: withhold criticism, generate as many ideas as possible, combine and extend ideas, and encourage freewheeling.

If your brainstorming gets bogged down, don't get discouraged and don't abandon the process until you have tried to restimulate yourself. Prod yourself by agreeing to stay with the process for another five minutes or so. Ask yourself if you can piggyback any other ideas or extend any of the ideas already generated. Reread the list you have generated and see if your ideas will stimulate additional ones.

After you have generated a sizable list, a period that should not take more than about 15 minutes, review the list and begin to evaluate the suggestions. Cross off the ones that are unworkable or that do not meet the criteria identified earlier.

The Idea Generator   This system consists of a dictionary of general topics and a series of questions that you can ask of any subject. The dictionary of topics in Figure 2.2 is an alphabetical listing of subjects in which each topic is broken down into several subtopics. These subtopics should begin to suggest potential subjects for your informative and persuasive speeches.

The topics portion comes from the system of topics (called *topoi*) used in the classical rhetorics of ancient Greece and Rome. The method consists of asking a series of questions about your general subject. Let's say you want to give a speech on homelessness. Applying the system of topics, you would ask such questions as the following:

- *Who* are the homeless?
- *Who* is the typical homeless person?
- *Who* is responsible for the increase in homelessness?
- *What* does it mean to be homeless?
- *What* does homelessness do to the people themselves?
- *What* does homelessness do to the society in general?
- *Why* are there so many homeless people?
- *Why* did this happen?
- *Why* is homelessness such an important social problem?
- *Why* must we be concerned with homelessness?
- *When* did homelessness become so prevalent?
- *Where* is homelessness most prevalent?
- *Where* is there an absence of homelessness?
- *How* can we help the homeless?
- *How* can we prevent others from becoming homeless?

These questions should be helpful to you in using these general topics to generate more specific ideas for your speeches. Try this method on any one of the topics listed in the dictionary portion of this idea generator. You'll be amazed at how many topics you will come up with. Your problem will quickly change from "What can I speak on?" to "Which one of these should I speak on?"

Art/Music/Theater Topics

Abstract art: meaning of; and emotion; leading artists; Kandinsky; Léger; Mondrian; Picasso; Pollock; contributions of movement; values of

Entertainment: industry; benefits; abuses; tax; functions of; and communication

Movies: censorship; famous; making; producing; directing; acting in; history of; economics of; career training; and communication

Music: festivals; forms; instruments; composition; styles; drama; opera; rock; punk; disco; country-western; popular; symphonic; new wave

Theater: Greek, Roman: commedia dell'arte; American; British; Eastern; Italian; French; performers; styles of; and television; and film; Broadway; and critics

Biological-Physiological Topics

Anesthesia: nature of; types of; uses of; development of; dangers of

Biological: clock; control; warfare; rhythm; sciences

Biorhythm: nature of; predictions from; life cycles; charting

Brain: -washing; damage; genius; intelligence; aphasia

Diseases: major diseases of college students; prevention; detection; treatment

Food: health; preservatives; additives; red dye; and allergies; preparation

Medicine: preventive; forensic; and health insurance; history of; and poisoning

Nutrition: nature of; functions of food; essential requirements; animal; human; and starvation; and diet; vitamins

Transplants: nature of; rejection; donor selection; legal aspects; ethical aspects; religious aspects; future of; advances in

Communication Topics

Advertising: techniques; expenditures; ethical; unethical; subliminal; leading agencies

Freedom of speech: laws protecting; and Constitution; significance of; abuses of; and censorship; and economics

Languages: artificial; sign; natural; learning of; loss of; pathologies of; sociology of; psychology of; international

Media: forms of; contributions of; abuses; regulation of; popularity of; influences of; and violence; and censorship; Nielsen ratings

Television: development of; history of; workings of; satellite; cable; commercials; propaganda; and leisure time; programming; economics

Translation: computer; missionary impetus; problems in; history of

Writing: styles; forms of; calligraphy; graphology; development of; and speech

Economic Topics

Business: cycles; associations; law; in performing arts; finance

Capitalism: nature of; economics of; development of; depression and inflation

Corporation: law; business; nature of; history; growth of the

Inflation: and deflation; causes of; effects of; types of

Investment: stocks; gold; real estate; art; restrictions on; bank; allowance

Taxation: alcohol; cigarette; history of; purposes of; historical methods of; types of

Treasury Department: monetary system; origin; functions of; and counterfeiting

Wealth: economic; distribution of; primitive economic systems; contemporary view

Continued on p. 14

FIGURE 2.2 A dictionary of topics.

Philosophical Topics

Empiricism: radical; nature of; doctrines; opposition to

Existentialism: meaning of; and choice; history of; leaders in; movement

Occultism: theories of; practices; rituals; astrology; theosophy; witchcraft; divination

Phenomenology: characteristics of; principles of; growth of; development of

Relativism: philosophy; ethical; meaning of; leaders of; influence

Religion: different religions; leaders in; influence of; beliefs and agnosticism

Witchcraft: meaning of; white and black; and magic; structure of; functions of; theories of; in primitive societies; in contemporary societies

Zen: meaning of; principles of; historical development of; contemporary interest in; teachings of; influence of

Political Topics

Amnesty: in draft evasion; in criminal law; and pardons; in Vietnam War

Communism: development of; theories of; religion and; ideologies

Government: federal; state; city; powers of; abuses of; types of; democracy; socialism; communism

Imperialism: nature of; economics of; problems with; practices; history

Nationalism: nature of; history of; philosophy of; chauvinism; self-determination

Supreme Court: judicial review; decisions; makeup of; chief justices; jurisdiction

United Nations (UN): development of; functions of; agencies; and League of Nations; structure of; veto powers; Security Council

War: conduct of; financing; destruction by; causes of; debts; games; casualties

Psychological Topics

Aggression: aggressive behavior in animals; in human beings; as innate; as learned

Alcohol: alcoholism; nature of; Alcoholics Anonymous; Al Anon; physical effects of; among the young; treatment of alcoholism

Autism: nature of; treatment for; symptoms; causes

Depression: nature of; and suicide; among college students; dealing with

Guilt: causes of; symptoms of; dealing with; effects of; and suicide; and religion

Intelligence: quotient; tests; theories of; cultural differences; measuring

Love: nature of; theories of; romantic; family; and hate; and interpersonal relationships; of self; and materialism

Personality: development of; measurement of; theories of; disorders

Sociological Topics

Cities: problems of; population patterns; and crime; movement into and out of

Crime: prevention; types of; and law; and punishment

Divorce: rate; throughout world; causes of; advantages of; disadvantages of; proceedings; traumas associated with

Ethnicity: measuring of; and prejudice; theories of; and culture

Feminism: meaning of; implications of; changing concepts of; and chauvinism

Gay: rights; life-style; laws against; prejudice against; and religion; and lesbian; statistics; relationships

Prison: reform; systems; security; routine; effect on crime; personality; behavior

Racism: nature of; self-hatred; genetic theory; human rights; education; religious

Suicide: causes; among college students; laws regulating; methods; aiding the suicide of another; philosophical implications; and religion

ESTABLISHING YOUR PURPOSE

The purpose of your speech is your objective, your goal; it is what you hope to achieve during your speech. It identifies the effect that you want your speech to have on your audience. In constructing your speech, first identify your general purpose, and then concentrate on your specific purpose.

General Purposes

The two major purposes of public speeches are to inform and persuade. In the *informative speech* you seek to create understanding: to clarify, to enlighten, to correct misunderstandings, or to demonstrate how something works. In this type of speech you rely most heavily on materials that amplify—examples, illustrations, definitions, testimony, audiovisual aids, and the like (see Chapter 6).

In the *persuasive speech*, which also presents information, you try to influence attitudes or behaviors. You seek to strengthen or change the existing attitudes or to get the audience to take some action. In this type of speech you rely heavily on materials that offer proof—evidence, argument, psychological appeals, and credibility appeals (see Chapter 6).

Specific Purposes

After you have established your general purpose, identify your specific purpose, which states more precisely what you aim to accomplish. For example, in an informative speech, your specific purpose identifies what you want to inform your audience about. Here are a few examples on the topic of informing an audience about AIDS:

General Purpose:	to inform
Specific Purposes:	to inform my audience of the recent progress in AIDS research
	to inform my audience of our college's plans for AIDS Awareness Day
	to inform my audience of the currently used tests for HIV infection

In a persuasive speech, your specific purpose identifies what you want your audience to believe, think, or do. Here are a few examples, again on the topic of AIDS:

General Purpose:	to persuade
Specific Purposes:	to persuade my audience to contribute to AIDS research
	to persuade my audience that they should be tested for HIV infection
	to persuade my audience to become better informed about how AIDS is transmitted

In formulating your specific purpose, keep the following guidelines in mind:

Use an infinitive phrase that elaborates on your general purpose. Both your general- and your specific-purpose statements should begin with the word *to* followed by *inform* or *persuade,* or perhaps *strengthen listeners' beliefs* or *change audience's attitude.*

Limit your specific purpose to one main point. Avoid trying to accomplish too much in too short a time. For example, "to inform my audience about the development of AIDS and the recent testing procedures for HIV infection" is actually two specific purposes. Select either one and build your speech around it. Beware of specific purposes that contain the word *and;* it's almost always a sign that you have two rather than one purpose.

Phrase your specific purpose with precise terms. The more precise your specific purpose, the more effectively it will guide you in the remaining steps of preparing your speech. Compare, for example, the following specific purpose statements:

    A.   to inform my audience about AIDS research
    B.   to inform my audience about recent advances in testing for HIV infection

Note how much more specific the "B" purpose is. The "A" statement merely identifies the general topic area; it does not identify what you hope to accomplish in your speech.

Limit your specific purpose to what you can reasonably accomplish in the time you have available. Remember that you have time limitations; you can only accomplish so much. Specific purposes that are too broad are useless. Such purposes as "to inform my audience about the world economy" or "to persuade my audience to improve their health" are too general.

"To inform my audience of the proposed European monetary system" or "to persuade my audience to exercise at least three times a week" are more limited and hence more appropriate.

ANALYZING YOUR AUDIENCE

CHAPTER OUTLINE

Seeking Audience Information
   Caution: All Generalizations Are False

Analyzing Audience Characteristics
   Age
   Gender
   Cultural Factors
   Educational and Intellectual Levels
   Occupation, Income, and Status
   Religion
   Other Factors

Analyzing Context Characteristics
   Size of the Audience
   The Physical Environment
   The Occasion
   Time of the Speech
   The Sequence of Events

Analyzing Psychological Characteristics
   Adapting to the Unwilling Audience
   Adapting to the Unfavorably Disposed Audience
   Adapting to Knowledgeable and Unknowledgeable Audiences
   Adapting to the Heterogeneous Audience

Analysis and Adaption During the Speech
   Speak Extemporaneously
   Focus on Listeners as Message Senders
   Address Audience Responses Directly

After completing this chapter, you should be able to

1. identify and use the four methods for seeking audience information

2. analyze and adapt to a wide variety of audiences

3. analyze and adapt to a variety of context characteristics

4. analyze and adapt to unwilling, unfavorable, knowledgeable, unknowledgeable, and heterogeneous audiences

5. analyze and adapt to audience responses during the speech

"People have one thing in common," noted Robert Zend. "They are all different." Because of these differences you need to analyze and adapt your speech to your specific, unique audience.

SEEKING AUDIENCE INFORMATION

The most effective way to learn about your audience's attitudes and beliefs is to analyze the audience's demographic or sociological characteristics. You can seek out audience information using a variety of methods: observation, data collection, interviewing, and inference (Sprague & Stuart, 1992).

Observe How do the members of your audience dress? Can you infer their possible economic status from their clothing and jewelry? Might their clothing reveal any conservative or liberal leanings? Might clothing provide clues to attitudes on economics or politics? What do they do in their free time? Where do they live? What do they talk about?

Collect Data Systematically Use a questionnaire to collect information before your speech. Let's say you took a course in desktop publishing and are thinking about giving an informative speech on the nature of desktop publishing. One thing you would need to know is how much your audience already knows. This would help you judge the level on which to approach the topic, what information you could assume, terms you would have to define, and so on. You might also want to know if the audience has ever seen documents produced by desktop publishing. If they haven't, examples would provide interesting visual aids.

Audience questionnaires are even more useful as background for your persuasive speeches. Let's say you plan to give a speech in favor of allowing single people to adopt children. To develop an effective speech, you would need to know your audience's attitudes toward single-parent adoption. Are they in favor of it? Opposed? If they have reservations, what are they? To help you answer such questions, you might use a questionnaire such as that presented in Figure 3.1.

1. How do you feel about single people adopting children?
_____ strongly in favor of it
_____ in favor of it
_____ neutral
_____ opposed to it
_____ strongly opposed to it

2. Is your attitude the same for interracial adoption? For gays and lesbians adopting? Please explain.

3. What is your main reason for or against single-parent adoption?

FIGURE 3.1 Audience questionnaire.

Interview a Few Members of Your Intended Audience In a classroom situation, this is easy to do. If you are to speak with an audience you will not meet prior to your speech, you might interview those who know the audience members better than you do. For example, you might talk with the person who invited you to speak.

If you do survey your audience—with a questionnaire or by interview—be sure to mention this in your speech. It will remind your listeners of your thoroughness and your concern for them. It will also satisfy their curiosity, as most people will be interested in how others responded.

Use "Intelligent Inference and Empathy" Try to adopt the perspective of the audience by using your knowledge of human behavior and human motivation. For example, if you are addressing recovering alcoholics, you might infer that your listeners have known both low and high self-esteem, that they have had experience in dealing with conflicts, and that they have a determination to take control of their own lives. Of course, you may be wrong about some of your listeners; but you can almost always make some reasonable inferences.

Caution: All Generalizations Are False
The generalizations noted here seem true in most cases but may not hold for any specific audience. *Beware of using these generalizations as stereotypes*. Don't assume that all men or all older people or all highly educated people think or believe the same things. They do not. Nevertheless, there are characteristics that seem to be more common in one group than another. And it is these characteristics that we attempt to capture in these generalizations. Use them to stimulate your thinking about your specific and unique audience. Most important, test what is said here against your own experience.

ANALYZING AUDIENCE CHARACTERISTICS

Let's look at the six sociological or demographic variables covered in *Human Communication* and how you might adapt to these differences.

Age
Take a specific example: You're an investment counselor and you want to persuade your listeners to invest their money to increase their earnings. You might begin your speech to an audience of retired persons in their 60s as follows:

> I want to talk with you about investing for your future. Now, I know what you're thinking. You're thinking to yourself, our future is now. You're thinking that you need more income now, not in the future. Well, that is what investing is all about. It's about increasing your income now, tomorrow, and next week and next month. Let me show you what I mean.

In your speech to young executives in their 30s, you might begin with something like this:

> I want to talk with you about investing for your future. In twenty years—years that will pass very quickly—many of you will be retiring. You will quickly learn that your company pension plan will prove woefully inadequate. Social Security will be equally inadequate. With only these sources of income you will have to lower your standard of living drastically. But that needn't happen. In fact, with extremely small investments made now and throughout your high-income–earning years, you will actually be able to live at a much higher standard than you ever thought possible.

Note that in both of these examples the speaker made inferences about the audience's attitudes toward investments on the basis of their age. The speaker demonstrated a knowledge of the audience and their immediate concerns. As a listener hearing even these brief excerpts you would feel that the speaker is addressing you directly and specifically. As a result you would probably give this speaker more attention than you'd give to one who spoke in generalities and without any clear idea of who was listening.

Graduating from college, achieving corporate success, raising a family, and saving for retirement are concerns that differ greatly from one age group to another. Learn your audience's goals. Know what they think about and care about. Connect your propositions and your supporting materials to these goals and concerns.

Will the age of your listeners influence their willingness to respond to appeals for liberal causes, to help the poor with welfare and housing, to invest in education, or to reform our prison system? Will age influence the importance they place on money, security, status, or family?

Might appeals to discovery, exploration, newness, and change find a more receptive hearing among the young? Might appeals to tradition be more appropriate for an older audience?

Gender

Traditionally, men have been found to place greater importance on theoretical, economic, and political values. Traditionally, women have been found to place greater importance on aesthetic, social, and religious values (Bem, 1974, 1981; Canary & Hause, 1993). In framing appeals and in selecting examples, use the values your audience members consider most important.

Men and women do not, for example, respond in the same way to such topics as abortion, rape, equal pay for equal work, and sexual harassment. Select your topics and supporting materials in light of the gender of your audience members. When your audience is mixed, make a special effort to relate "women's" topics to men and "men's" topics to women.

Relational topics—for example, friendship, love, and family—are popular with women but less so with men. (Simply picking up a random selection of magazines targeted to women and those targeted to men provides evidence of this tendency. Look at the advertisements, the articles, and even the cartoons.) When speaking on these topics to women, you will probably find a receptive audience. When speaking on such topics to men, draw explicit connections between these topics and their values, needs, and interests.

Cultural Factors

Speakers who fail to demonstrate an understanding of cultural differences will be distrusted. Speakers, especially those who are seen to be outsiders, who imply that all African Americans are athletic and all lesbians are masculine will quickly lose credibility. Avoid any implication that you are stereotyping audience members (or groups to which they belong). It is sure to work against your achieving your purpose.

For example, the degree to which listeners are loyal to family members, feel responsibility for the aged, and believe in the value of education will vary from one culture to another. Build your appeals around *your* audience's attitudes, beliefs, and values.

Educational and Intellectual Levels

Generally, the educated are more concerned with issues outside their immediate field of operation. They are concerned with international affairs, economic issues, and the broader philosophical and sociological issues confronting the nation and the world. The educated recognize that these issues affect them in many ways. Often the uneducated do not see the connection. Therefore, when speaking to a less-educated audience, draw the connections explicitly and relate such topics to their more immediate concerns.

The more educated will probably be less swayed by appeals to emotion and to authority. They will be more skeptical of generalizations (as you should be of my generalizations in this chapter). They will question the validity of statistics and frequently demand better substantiation of your propositions. The educated are more likely to apply the tests of evidence discussed in Chapter 6.

As a speaker you will be able to assume more background knowledge when addressing an educated than an uneducated audience. Fill in the necessary background and detail for the less educated.

Occupation, Income, and Status

Appeal to these factors when appropriate and attack them only with extreme caution. Samuel Johnson put it this way: "The rights of nations, and of kings, sink into questions of grammar, if grammarians discuss them."

Higher-status people are generally more future-oriented (Gonzalez & Zimbardo, 1985). They train and plan for the future. Their goals are clear and their efforts are directly addressed to achieving these goals. Even their reading matter relates to these goals. For example, they read *Forbes, Fortune,* and *The Wall Street Journal* to help them achieve their financial goals. When speaking to a lower-status audience, relate future-oriented issues to their more immediate and present situation.

Religion

Religion permeates all topics and all issues. On a most obvious level, we know that such issues as birth control, abortion, gay and lesbian rights, and divorce are closely connected to religion. Similarly, premarital sex, marriage, child rearing, money, cohabitation, responsibilities toward parents, and thousands of other issues are clearly related to religion.

Religion is also important, however, in areas where its connection is not so obvious. For example, religion influences one's ideas concerning such topics as obedience to authority, responsibility to government, and the usefulness of such qualities as honesty, guilt, and happiness.

When dealing with any religious beliefs and particularly when disagreeing with them, recognize that you are going to meet stiff opposition. Proceed slowly and inductively; present your evidence and argument before expressing your disagreement.

Do not assume that a religious leader's opinion or pronouncement is accepted by the rank-and-file members. Generally, opinion polls demonstrate that official statements by religious leaders take a more conservative position and members are more liberal.

Other Factors

Always consider your audience's *expectations,* whether or not you intend to fulfill them. If your audience expects you to be humorous, you must either be humorous or explain why you won't be.

What is the *relational* status of your listeners? Are they married? Single? Divorced? Cohabitors? Widowed? Do the members wish to get married? Are they content in their present state, or do they wish to change in some way? Are they without primary relationships, or are they in such relationships?

What *special interests* do the audience members have? Do they have hobbies you might refer to? What occupies their leisure time? Are they interested in films? Television? Community projects? Sports?

Do the people in your audience have significant *organizational memberships*? Are they joiners? Nonjoiners? What organizations do they belong to? How might these organizations influence what you as a speaker might say or expect? Are they members of the NRA? The AMA? CORE? What does this mean for your speech development?

What are the major *political affiliations* of your listeners? Are they politically liberal? Conservative? Are they uninvolved and uninterested? What does this mean to the development of your speech?

ANALYZING CONTEXT CHARACTERISTICS

In addition to analyzing specific listeners, consider the specific context in which you will speak. Consider the size of the audience, the physical environment, the occasion, the time of your speech, and where your speech fits into the sequence of events.

Size of the Audience

How might the size of your audience influence your speech presentation? Generally, the larger the audience, the more formal the speech presentation should be. With a small audience, you may be more casual and informal. Also, the larger the audience is, the more differences there will be. In a large audience you will have a greater variety of religions, a greater range of occupations, a greater number of different income levels, and so on. Therefore, include supporting materials that will appeal to all members.

The Physical Environment

How will the physical environment influence your speech presentation? The physical environment—indoors or outdoors, room or auditorium, sitting or standing audience—is important.

Take a few minutes to erase or lessen the problem of entering the public speaking environment totally cold. Spend some time in front of the room. See the room from the perspective of the speaker, before you are ready to speak. Survey the entire room. Look at the windows, the back wall, the desks, the students, and so on. See the room the way you will as a speaker.

The Occasion

How might the occasion influence the nature and the reception of your speech? The type of occasion will dictate in part the kind of speech required. A wedding speech will differ drastically from a funeral speech, which will differ drastically from one at a political rally. The occasion influences what is appropriate in terms of topic, treatment, language, and all of the variables of public speaking. In constructing the speech, focus on each element in relation to the occasion. Ask yourself in what way the particular public speaking element (language, organization, supporting materials, for example) might be made more responsive to this particular occasion.

Time of the Speech

How might the time during which you are to give your speech influence your presentation? If you are to give your speech in an early morning class, say around eight o'clock, then take into consideration that some of your listeners will still be half asleep. Tell them you appreciate their being here. Compliment their attention. If necessary, wake them up with your voice, gestures, attention-gaining materials, visual aids, and the like. If your speech is in the evening, when most of your listeners are anxious to get home, recognize this as well.

The Sequence of Events

Where does your speech fit into the sequence of events? A useful procedure is to scan a recent newsmagazine as well as the morning newspaper to see if any items relate to what you will say in your speech. If so, you might make reference to the story as a way of gaining attention, adding support to your argument, or stressing the importance of the topic.

Also consider where your speech fits in with the other speeches that will be heard that day or during that class. If you are to speak after one or more other speakers, try especially hard to build in some reference to a previous speech. This will help to stress your similarity with the audience members and will also help you demonstrate important connections between what you are saying and what others have said.

ANALYZING PSYCHOLOGICAL CHARACTERISTICS

Let's consider how you might adapt to such varied audiences as the unwilling, the unfavorable, the knowledgeable, the unknowledgeable, and the heterogeneous.

Adapting to the Unwilling Audience

The unwilling audience demands special and delicate handling. Here are a few suggestions to help change your listeners from unwilling to willing.

Secure their interest and attention as early in your speech as possible. Reinforce this throughout the speech. Use little-known facts, quotations, startling statistics, examples and illustrations, audiovisual aids, and the like. These devices will help you secure and maintain the attention of an initially unwilling audience.

Reward the audience for their attendance and attention. Do this in advance of your main arguments. Let the audience know you are aware they are making a sacrifice in coming to hear you speak. Tell them you appreciate it. One student, giving a speech close to midterm time, said simply:

> I know how easy it is to cut classes during midterm time to finish the unread chapters and do everything else you have to do. So I especially appreciate your being here this morning. What I have to say, however, will interest you and will be of direct benefit to all of you.

Once acknowledged, it is difficult for an audience to continue to feel unwilling.

Relate your topic and supporting materials directly to your audience's needs and wants. Show your listeners how they can save time, make more money, solve their problems, or become more popular. If you fail to do this, then your audience has a good reason for not listening.

Adapting to the Unfavorably Disposed Audience

Build on commonalities; emphasize not the differences but the similarities. Stress what you and the audience share as people, as interested citizens, as fellow students. Here, for example, Alan Nelson (1986) identifies with the city of his audience in his introduction:

> Returning to the Golden Gate, my home area, reminds me of another harbor and a beautiful statue. . . . The Statue of Liberty, which has stood for 100 years in New York Harbor, is being rededicated this year and represents the heritage of America.

Build your speech from areas of agreement, through areas of slight disagreement, up to the major differences. Always proceed in small steps. Let's say you represent management. You wish to persuade employees of your factory to accept a particular wage offer. You might begin with such areas of agreement as the mutual desire for improved working conditions or for economic growth. In any disagreement or argument, there are still areas of agreement. Emphasize these.

Strive for small gains. Do not try to convince a pro-life group to contribute money for the new abortion clinic or a pro-choice group to vote against liberalizing abortion laws in a five-minute speech. Be content to get them to see some validity to your position and to listen fairly. About-face changes take a long time to achieve. To attempt too much persuasion, too much change, can only result in failure or resentment.

Adapting to Knowledgeable and Unknowledgeable Audiences

Treat audiences that lack knowledge of the topic very carefully. Never confuse a lack of knowledge with a lack of an ability to understand.

Do not talk down to these members of your audience. This is perhaps the greatest communication error that teachers make. After having taught a subject for years, they face, semester after semester, students who have no knowledge of the topic. As a result, many teachers often talk down to the audience and, in the process, lose them. No one wants to listen to a speaker putting him or her down.

Do not confuse a lack of knowledge with a lack of intelligence. An audience may have no knowledge of your topic but be quite capable of following a clearly presented, logically developed argument. Try especially hard to use concrete examples, audiovisual aids, and simple language. Fill in background details as required. Avoid jargon and specialized terms that may be clear to you but would not be to someone new to the subject.

Audiences with much knowledge also require special handling, because their response may well be, "Why should I listen to this? I already know about this topic."

Let the audience know that you are aware of their knowledge and expertise. And try to do this as early in the speech as possible. Emphasize that what you have to say will not be redundant. Tell them that you will be presenting recent developments or new approaches. In short, let them know that they will not be wasting their time listening to your speech.

Emphasize your credibility, especially your competence in this general subject area (see Chapter 6). Let the audience know that you have earned the right to speak. Let them know that what you have to say is based on a firm grasp of the material.

Adapting to the Heterogeneous Audience

The greater the homogeneity of the audience, the easier will be your analysis and adaptation. There will also be less chance of making serious mistakes as a speaker. Consider an audience whose members are all middle-aged men working in nonunion sweat shops, earning the minimum wage. They all share the same religion and cultural background and they all have less than an eighth-grade education. This audience—albeit to an unrealistic extreme—is homogeneous. The members share a number of important characteristics. So, it will be relatively easy to analyze and adapt to them.

On the other hand, a heterogeneous audience will require a much more complex audience analysis and a much more careful plan of adaptation. Consider, for example, a PTA audience composed of parents, differing widely in income and education, and teachers, differing widely in background, training, and age. Each of these groups will have different points of view, backgrounds, and expectations. As a speaker you will have to recognize these differences and take special care to appeal to all groups.

When the audience is too heterogeneous, it is sometimes helpful to subdivide it and appeal to each section separately. A common example is the audience consisting of men and women. Say the topic is abortion on demand. To limit yourself to arguments that would appeal equally to men and women might seriously damage your case. Consider, therefore, concentrating first on arguments that women can relate to and then on those that men can relate to. You thus avoid using supporting materials that fall in between the groups and that are effective with neither.

Homogeneity does not equal attitudinal sameness. The audience that is similar in age, sex, educational background, and so on, will probably also share similar attitudes and beliefs. However, this is not always true. Heterogeneity increases with the size of the group. As any group expands in size, their characteristics become more diverse. Keep this in mind when you are analyzing your audiences.

For example, college professors would probably be more liberal on many social and political issues than would, say, farmers. However, as the group of college professors increases in size, their liberalness will approach a bell-shaped curve. A small percentage will be extremely liberal and another small percentage will be extremely conservative. The majority, however, will be somewhere in between. This does not mean that this bell-shaped curve will be the same as that for Midwestern farmers. It does mean that within each group there will be a diversity that will increase with the size of the group.

The speaker who ignores this simple truism—speakers who assume that all college students enjoy reading, that all Catholics are against abortion, or that all parents want to be parents—is sure to encounter difficulties. The speaker is likely to be perceived as an outsider who really doesn't understand the group and especially the group's diversity. The audience may feel they are being stereotyped. These difficulties are compounded when such generalizations are based on race and nationality because these stereotypes often engender resentment and may even be perceived as racist.

ANALYSIS AND ADAPTATION DURING THE SPEECH

In your classroom speeches, you will face a known audience, an audience you have already analyzed and to which you have made appropriate adaptations. At other times, however, you may face an audience that you have not been able to analyze beforehand or one that differs greatly from the audience you thought you would address. In these cases you will have to analyze and adapt to them as you speak. Here are a variety of suggestions for making this process easier and more effective.

Speak Extemporaneously

As we explain in detail in Chapter 10, when you speak extemporaneously, you write into the delivery outline your main assertions and your supporting materials—in the order in which they will be spoken. However, you avoid memorizing your speech or committing yourself to the exact wording you will use. This method provides you with great flexibility to delete examples that may be inappropriate or to add examples that may be more relevant to this new audience.

The key here is to avoid memorizing your speech; if you do, you will find it impossible to make these essential last-minute adjustments.

Focus on Listeners as Message Senders

As you are speaking, look at your listeners as speakers. Remember that public speaking is a transactional process; just as you are sending messages to your audience, they are also sending messages to you. Just as they are responding to what you are communicating, you need to respond to what they are communicating. Pay attention to these messages and on the basis of what these tell you, make the necessary adjustments.

There are a wide variety of adjustments that could be made to each type of audience response. Here are just a few suggestions to start you thinking. For example, if your audience shows signs of boredom, you might increase your volume, move closer to them, or tell them that what you are going to say will be of value to them. If your audience shows signs of disagreement or hostility, you might stress some similarity you have with them. If your audience looks puzzled, you might pause a moment and rephrase your ideas, provide necessary definitions, or insert an internal summary. If your audience seems impatient, you might say, "My last argument . . . ," instead of your originally planned "My third argument. . . ."

Address Audience Responses Directly

Another way of dealing with such responses is to confront them directly and say to those who disagree, for example:

> I know you disagree with this position, but all I ask is that you hear me out and see if this new way of doing things will not simplify your accounting procedures.

Or to those who seem puzzled, you might say:

> I know this plan may seem confusing, but bear with me; it will become clear in a moment.

Or to those who seem impatient, you might respond:

> I know this has been a long day, but give me just a few more minutes and you'll be able to save hours recording your accounts.

By responding to your listeners' responses, you acknowledge their needs. You let them know that you hear them, that you are with them, and that you are responding to their very real concerns.

CHAPTER 4

RESEARCHING YOUR SPEECH

CHAPTER CONTENTS

General Principles of Research
    Examine What You Know
    Work from the General to the Specific
    Take Accurate Notes
    Use Research Time Effectively
    Learn the Available Resources

Sources for Research
    The Experts
    The Book Catalog
    Encyclopedias
    Biographical Material
    Newspaper, Magazine, and Journal Indexes
    Almanacs
    Government Publications

Researching Online
    Databases

Integrating Research into Your Speech

CHAPTER GOALS

After completing this chapter, you should be able to

1. follow the general principles of research

2. access a wide variety of printed research sources

3. access a variety of computerized databases

Suppose you are to speak to your class on surrogate motherhood. Where do you go for information? How can you learn about the number of surrogate mothers? How do you discover the procedures involved for securing a surrogate mother? What are the legal issues involved? What were the prominent legal battles? Research will enable you to answer these and hundreds of other questions.

In this chapter, we examine research and explain how you can go about the process of answering your questions—regardless of the topic—efficiently and effectively. We present research in three parts. First, we focus on some general principles to follow in conducting research. Second, we look at some useful research sources and the new developments in computer research. And finally, we offer some suggestions for integrating research into your speech.

An essential part of the research process is your evaluation of the information and argument that you do locate. For example, you will want to use information that is recent (rather than dated) and objective (rather than biased). These and related issues are covered in our discussions of amplifying materials and argument (Chapter 6).

GENERAL PRINCIPLES OF RESEARCH

These general principles will help you throughout your entire college and professional career. You will always need to find information, so here are some ways to handle this task more efficiently and effectively.

Examine What You Know

Begin your search by examining what you already know. Write down, for example, any books or articles on the topic or persons who might know something about the topic. This way you can attack the problem systematically and not waste effort and time.

Work from the General to the Specific

Get a general overview of the topic first. An encyclopedia or journal article will serve this purpose well, helping you see the topic as a whole and how its various parts fit together. After securing this overview, consult increasingly specific and specialized source materials.

Take Accurate Notes

The more accurate your notes are, the less time you will waste going back to sources to check on a date or spelling. Accurate records will also prevent you from going to sources you have already consulted but may have forgotten.

Key your notes to the topics in your preliminary speech outline. For example, suppose your speech is to be on surrogate motherhood. Your preliminary outline looks like this:

Surrogate Motherhood
  I. Legal aspects
  II. Moral aspects
  III. Psychological aspects

You might then classify your notes under these three major topics. Simply head the card or page with legal, moral, or psychological. Because this is a preliminary outline, you will need a large miscellaneous category for information that doesn't fit any of your preestablished categories.

Use Research Time Effectively

If you are going to give two speeches on the same topic, do the research for both at the same time. Don't wait until you have finished the first speech to begin researching the second. You might, for example, divide a looseleaf notebook into two sections and insert material into one section with appropriate cross-references in the other.

Learn the Available Resources

When you know how to research, it will be easy, pleasant, and rewarding. When you lack this information, research throughout your college and professional career will be hateful and wasteful. Learn what is available, where, and how. Spend a few hours in the library learning where some of the most useful source materials are located.

- Where are the encyclopedias? The almanacs? The indexes?
- Where are newspapers and journals located?
- What material is on microfilm?
- How does your library operate interlibrary loans?
- What other libraries are available in your area? Are there municipal or college libraries that might complement your college library?
- What computer search facilities are available?

SOURCES FOR RESEARCH

More than 30 million different books have been published since the printing process was invented. Currently, approximately 400,000 titles are published each year. Millions of articles are published each year in thousands of different journals and magazines. There are now more than 100,000 journals and magazines in the area of science alone.

The information currently available on just about any topic is so vast that it is understandably daunting for many people. Here we try to make the initial search procedure easier and less forbidding by identifying some significant sources of information.

The Experts

The faculty is one of the best, if rarely used, sources of information for almost any speech topic. Regardless of what your topic is, someone on the faculty of some department knows a great deal about the topic. At the least, they will be able to direct you to appropriate sources.

Experts in the community can serve similar functions. Local politicians, religious leaders, doctors, lawyers, museum directors, and the like are often suitable sources of information. If you plan on interviewing such people, follow the guidelines for information interviews provided in Unit 15 of *Human Communication*.

Another obvious expert is the librarian at your college or local library. Librarians know the contents and mechanics of libraries; they are experts in the very issues that may be giving you trouble. Librarians will be able to help you in finding biographical material, indexes of current articles, materials in specialized collections at other libraries, and so on. Use the librarian as a resource person to help you locate the right materials in the shortest possible time.

The Book Catalog

Each library catalogs its books in a slightly different way, depending on its size and the needs of its users. All, however, make use of some form of catalog. If your library uses the traditional card or book catalog, you will find three types of cards or books: title, subject, and author. Thus, if you know the title or the author of the book you want, go to those cards or that volume where the book is located. If you have just a general subject heading, use subject headings. These identify all the books your library has on this subject.

Other libraries have their catalog online (computerized), a system most libraries are moving toward. Online systems allow you to use a computer terminal to find the location of desired books. Usually, you may search the library's contents using title, author, or subject matter identifiers. This system is extremely easy to use and even tells you the book's present status, for example, if it is on reserve or on loan and when it's due back.

Encyclopedias

One of the best places to start to investigate your topic is a standard encyclopedia. You will get a general overview of the subject and suggestions for additional reading. The most comprehensive and the most prestigious is the *Encyclopaedia Britannica* (32 volumes). The annual *Britannica Book of the Year* updates the encyclopedia as a whole.

Collier's Encyclopedia, the *Encyclopedia Americana*, and the *Academic American Encyclopedia* are also excellent and comprehensive. These works provide much insight into just about any subject you might look up.

The many specialized encyclopedias may also be helpful. *The New Catholic Encyclopedia* (15 volumes) is the best and most scholarly source for general information on the Catholic Church. *Encyclopedia Judaica* (16 volumes plus yearbooks) emphasizes Jewish life and includes biographies and detailed coverage of the Jewish contribution to world culture. *Encyclopedia of Islam* and *Encyclopedia of Buddhism* cover the development, beliefs, institutions, and personalities of Islam and Buddhism. For information on the physical, applied, and natural sciences, refer to the 20-volume *McGraw-Hill Encyclopedia of Science and Technology,* which is complemented by an annual supplement, the *McGraw-Hill Yearbook of Science and Technology*. *Our Living World of Nature* is a 14-volume popular encyclopedia dealing with natural history from an ecological point of view. The *International Encyclopedia of the Social Sciences* concentrates on the theory and methods of the social sciences in 17 well-researched volumes. Other widely used encyclopedias include the *Encyclopedia of Bioethics* (4 volumes), the *Encyclopedia of Philosophy* (8 volumes), and the *Encyclopedia of Religion* (16 volumes).

Some encyclopedias, such as *Compton's Multimedia Encyclopedia* and *Grolier,* are now available on CD-ROM (compact disk, read-only memory), a computerized database we consider in detail in the next section. This system allows you to locate articles, maps, diagrams, and even definitions of difficult terms (through the built-in dictionary) easily and efficiently. To locate articles, simply type in the terms that describe the topic you want to explore.

Biographical Material

A speaker often needs information about particular individuals. Consult the *Biography Index* first. It contains an index to biographies appearing in various sources— magazines, books, letters, and diaries. This work is particularly useful for locating information on living persons who have not yet been the subject of thorough biographies.

The *Dictionary of American Biography* (DAB), modeled after the British *Dictionary of National Biography*, contains articles on famous deceased Americans from all areas of accomplishment. For living individuals the best single source is *Current Biography*. This is issued monthly and in cumulative annual volumes. Published since 1940, *Current Biography* contains articles of one to two pages in length, most with photographs and brief bibliographies. The essays in *Current Biography* are written by an editorial staff. The entries in *Who's Who in America*, which also covers living individuals, are compiled from questionnaires returned by the subjects covered.

In addition, there are a host of other more specialized works whose titles indicate their scope. *Directory of American Scholars* contains biographies of many of your teachers as well as scholars throughout the United States and Canada. Others include the *International Who's Who, Who Was Who in America, Who's Who* (primarily British), *Dictionary of Scientific Biography, American Men and Women of Science, Great Lives from History* (25 volumes), *Notable American Women, National Cyclopedia of American Biography* (1888–1984), *Who's Who in the Arab World, Who's Who in the World, Who's Who in Finance and Industry, Who's Who in American Politics, Who's Who Among Black Americans, Who's Who of American Women,* and *Who's Who Among Hispanic Americans.* For every group of people there seems to be a suitable and comprehensive biographical sourcebook.

Newspaper, Magazine, and Journal Indexes

Indexes to the various newspapers, magazines, and professional journals are extremely useful.

Newspaper Indexes *The New York Times Index,* published since 1913, is important because it indexes one of the leading newspapers in the world. The newspaper is widely available and carefully indexed. It enables you to locate important news stories; book, play, and movie reviews; sports accounts; obituaries; complete texts of important speeches; and political, economic, and social commentaries. It also contains brief summaries of major news items and lists the major events in chronological order. Also useful is *The Wall Street Journal Index,* published since 1958. This indexes the most important newspaper for financial and business news. The *National Newspaper Index,* published since 1972, indexes such newspapers as the *Chicago Tribune,* the *Christian Science Monitor,* the *Los Angeles Times,* and the *Washington Post,* each of which has its own index.

Magazine Indexes The *Reader's Guide to Periodical Literature* covers magazine articles for the period from 1900 to the present. This guide indexes by subject and by author (in one convenient alphabetical index) articles published in some 180 different magazines. The *Abridged Reader's Guide* indexes about 60 publications and may prove more convenient than the longer version. *Reader's Guide* is valuable for its broad coverage, but it is limited in that it covers mostly general publications and only a few of the more specialized ones.

For more advanced materials, consult some of the more specific and specialized indexes noted below. Also, consult other indexes for other popular but perhaps less conservative periodicals. For example, *Reader's Guide* does not index such publications as *Mother Jones* and *Interview*. The *Popular Periodical Index*, published since 1973, indexes these and similar publications. The *Alternative Press Index*, published since 1970, indexes almost 200 magazines, newspapers, and journals that might be labeled "radical." This index is valuable for speakers dealing with such issues as the Third World, minority rights, socialism, and the like. *Access*, published since 1975, also indexes publications not covered in *Reader's Guide*.

The *Education Index,* published since 1929, indexes articles from about 330 journals and magazines relevant to education, including most communication journals and government periodicals. *The Social Sciences Index* covers periodicals in such areas as psychology, economics, sociology, and political science, and is especially useful for its cross-disciplinary coverage.

Journal Abstracts   In addition to these indexes, which are guides to locating material within a general subject area, there are many helpful abstracts. The most comprehensive is *Psychological Abstracts*, which provides short summaries of articles that appeared in psychology journals and books. It contains both subject and author indexes. *Sociological Abstracts, Linguistics and Language Behavior Abstracts*, and *Communication Abstracts* are other important sources.

Computerized Indexes and Abstracts   You will find computerized indexes and abstracts easier to use, although not all libraries have them. Many of these are available on CD-ROM (see Researching Online). For example, *Magazine Index Plus* is a computerized database that indexes over 400 magazines covering a wide variety of topics such as entertainment, travel, and current affairs. *Periodical Abstracts* contains indexes to over 250 magazines covered by *Reader's Guide to Periodical Literature*.

National Newspaper Index provides indexes to *The New York Times*, *The Wall Street Journal*, the *Christian Science Monitor*, the *Washington Post*, and the *Los Angeles Times*. *Newspaper Abstracts* contains indexes to the above papers as well as to the *Atlanta Constitution*, the *Chicago Tribune*, and the *Boston Globe*.

Almanacs

The best single source for information of all kinds is the almanac. Numerous inexpensive ones published annually are perhaps the most up-to-date source on many topics. The most popular are *The World Almanac & Book of Facts* and the *Information Please Almanac*. *Whitaker's Almanac* is the best of the British almanacs and *Canadian Almanac and Directory* is the best source for data on Canada and Canadians.

Government Publications

Here is just a small sampling of the publications that are available in most libraries or directly from the Government Printing Office in Washington, D.C.

The United States Bureau of the Census publishes *Statistical Abstract of the United States* (from 1878 to the present) and *Historical Statistics of the United States, Colonial Times to 1957* (with various supplements). Together these volumes contain the most complete information on immigration, economics, geography, education, population, and various other topics that has been collected during the various census counts. Other valuable statistical sources include *Vital Statistics of the United States* (especially useful for demographic statistics), *Morbidity and Mortality Weekly Report* (useful for health-related issues), and *Employment and Earnings* (useful for labor force statistics). For international statistics see *United Nations Statistical Yearbook*, *World Statistics in Brief*, and *UNESCO Statistical Yearbook*.

The *Official Congressional Directory* (1809 to date) and the *Biographical Directory of the American Congress* (1774–1961) contain biographical information on government personnel, maps of congressional districts, and other information helpful to those concerned with the workings of Congress.

The *Congressional Record* (1873 to date) contains all that was said in both houses of Congress as well as materials that members of Congress wish inserted.

RESEARCHING ONLINE

As noted, many of the indexes and abstracts formerly available only in print form are now available online (in which you access an "outside" database) and on CD-ROM (in which you access a database contained on high-density compact disks that have read-only memory). New indexes and journals are being added to these databases regularly. These systems enable you to access many of the indexes and abstracts discussed above. For example, *Psychological Abstracts, Sociological Abstracts, Humanities Index, Social Science Index,* and *ERIC* are available online and on CD-ROM. Some indexes are only available online or on CD-ROM, for example, ABI/INFORM and LEXIS/NEXIS, discussed below.

One great advantage to computerized research is that you don't have to copy each reference you find. Instead you can print out your search or download it to your own computer disk.

An even greater advantage of computerized searching is that it enables you to search for two or more concepts at the same time. For example, let's say you are giving a speech on the relationship between crime and drugs. In a manual search, you would have to go through all the entries on crime for those that linked crime with drugs. In some cases the titles of the articles would be unrevealing. You would therefore have to get the actual article to discover if it was relevant or not. This would take considerable time. With a computerized search you can specify that you want a search of only those references dealing with both crime *and* drugs. The computer will do the work for you. It will retrieve only those references directly related to your topic of the relationship of crime and drugs.

Some computerized searches provide a simple list of references. Others provide you with detailed abstracts of the information contained in the book or article.

Databases

When you do research through computer, you access a database. A database is simply information contained in one place. A dictionary, an encyclopedia, and an index to magazines are examples of databases. A computerized database is the same except that it is accessed through a computer. A variety of databases are now available. Through them you can avail yourself of a wide spectrum of reference materials.

For example, Dialog offers nearly 400 databases. One of the databases available from Dialog is *PsycINFO*. This database examines over 1,300 periodicals and technical reports each year that deal with just about every psychological issue imaginable. The *Linguistics and Language Behavior Abstracts* database contains references to studies on language. The *Social Scisearch* database covers the social and behavioral sciences. The *Legal Resource Index* covers those periodicals devoted to law. CompuServe (a subsidiary of H&R Block) contains such databases as *Grolier Encyclopedia* and general and business news services. The Source (a subsidiary of Reader's Digest Association) contains, for example, Associated Press and United Press International news services. ABI/INFORM Database covers more than 800 periodicals in business.

The LEXIS/NEXIS System allows you to retrieve the complete text of articles from hundreds of newspapers, magazines, journals, and even newsletters in addition to a wide variety of legal and statutory records.

There is probably a vendor and an appropriate database for just about any topic you can think of. Once you have selected your topic, you might wish to consult a directory of the available databases to locate the database that would be most appropriate for you. For example, *The CD-ROM Directory* contains over 1,500 databases. The *Directory of Online Databases* identifies about 2,500 databases throughout the world. In these directories, you would discover the particular database that would contain the area you wish to research. Librarians will be familiar with the various databases and you should avail yourself of their expertise.

Computerized searches vary in cost. Scientific databases are relatively expensive to access. Social science databases are relatively inexpensive. Some colleges will perform computer searches for faculty and graduate students but not for undergraduates. In most college libraries CD-ROM searches are free to all students.

Since computer search facilities vary so much from one school to another and since they are expanding so rapidly, it is best to consult your librarian.

INTEGRATING RESEARCH INTO YOUR SPEECH

Now that you have amassed this wealth of research material, here are a few suggestions for integrating it into your speech.

Mention the sources in your speech by citing at least the author and, if helpful, the publication and the date. Here is how C. Kenneth Orski (1986) did it:

> In assessing what the future may hold for transportation I will lean heavily on a technique pioneered by John Naisbitt, author of *Megatrends*. Naisbitt believes that the most reliable way to anticipate the future is to try to understand the present. To this end he methodologically scans 6,000 daily local newspapers from around the country.

Provide smooth transitions between your words and the words of the author you're citing. In this excerpt, Marilyn Loden (1986) does this most effectively:

> In his book, *Leadership*, James MacGregor Burns advocates new leadership styles which encourage employees to take more risk, to be more self-reliant and manage more creatively. He calls this new management approach "transformational leadership."

Avoid such expressions as "I have a quote here" or "I want to quote an example." Let the audience know that you are quoting by pausing before the quote, taking a step forward, or referring to your notes to read the extended quotation.

CHAPTER 5

DEVELOPING YOUR THESIS AND MAJOR PROPOSITIONS

CHAPTER CONTENTS

Your Thesis
    Using Thesis Statements
    Wording the Thesis
    A Note on Thesis and Purpose
Your Major Propositions
    Selecting and Wording Propositions
    Some Additional Guidelines

CHAPTER GOALS

After completing this chapter, you should be able to

1. identify an appropriate thesis for a public speech

2. generate main ideas from the thesis

3. word the thesis appropriately

4. select and word major propositions based on the thesis

Now that you have selected your topic and purpose and have researched your topic, you are ready to frame your thesis and develop your major propositions.

YOUR THESIS

Your first step is to write out your thesis statement. This is your main assertion, what you want the audience to absorb from your speech. The thesis of Lincoln's Second Inaugural Address was that Northerners and Southerners should work together for the entire nation's welfare. The thesis of the *Rocky* movies was that the underdog can win.

Let us say you are planning to deliver a speech supporting Senator Wainwright. Your thesis statement might be something like this: "We should support Wainwright's candidacy." This is what you want your audience to believe as a result of your speech. In an informative speech the thesis statement focuses on what you want your audience to learn as a result of your speech. For example, a thesis for a speech on jealousy might be: "There are two theories of jealousy."

Be sure to limit the thesis statement to one central idea. Statements such as "We should support Wainwright and the entire Democratic party" contain not one but two basic ideas.

Notice that in persuasive speeches, the thesis statement puts forth a point of view, an opinion. The thesis is an arguable, debatable proposition. It is nonneutral. In informative speeches, the thesis appears relatively neutral and objective. In many ways, however, it too states a point of view. Our example states that there are *two* theories of jealousy.

Using Thesis Statements

The thesis statement serves two useful purposes. First, it helps you generate your main ideas or assertions. Second, it focuses the audience's attention on your central idea.

Generating Main Ideas   Once you have phrased your thesis statement, the main divisions of your speech are readily suggested. Let's take an example: "The Webber bill will provide needed services for senior citizens." The obvious question to address in preparing a speech with this thesis is: *What are they?* The answer to this question suggests the main parts of your speech, for example, health, food, shelter, and recreational services. These four areas then become the four main points of your speech. An outline of the main ideas would look like this:

    I.   The Webber bill provides needed health services.
    II.   The Webber bill provides needed food services.
    III.   The Webber bill provides needed shelter services.
    IV.   The Webber bill provides needed recreational services.

The remainder of the speech would then be filled in with supporting materials (covered in Chapter 6 of this *Guide*). For example, you might identify the several needed health services and explain how the Webber bill provides for these services. This first main division of your speech might, in outline, look something like this:

    I.   The Webber bill provides needed health services.

A. Neighborhood clinics will be established.
B. Medical hot lines for seniors will be established.

In the completed speech this first major proposition and its two subordinate statements might be spoken like this:

> The Webber bill provides senior citizens with the health services they need so badly. Let me give you some examples of these badly needed health services. One of the most important services will be the establishment of neighborhood health clinics. Seven such clinics are already in the planning stages and will be established throughout the district. These clinics will help senior citizens get needed health advice and services right in their own neighborhoods.
>
> Another important health service will be the health hot lines. . . .

Focusing Audience Attention   The thesis sentence also focuses the audience's attention on your central idea. In some speeches you may wish to state your thesis early in your speech—in the introduction or perhaps early in the body of the speech. There are instances, however, when you may not want to state your thesis. Or you may want to state it late in your speech. For example, if your audience is hostile to your thesis, it may be wise to give your evidence and arguments first. In this way you will be able to move them gradually into a more positive frame of mind before stating your thesis.

In other cases, you may want the audience to infer your thesis without actually spelling it out. Beginning speakers especially should be careful in choosing not to state their thesis explicitly. Most audiences—and especially uneducated audiences—will not be persuaded by speeches in which the speaker does not explicitly state the thesis. Listeners often fail to grasp what the thesis is and so do not change their attitudes or behaviors.

Make your decision as to when (or if) to state your thesis on the basis of what will be more effective with your specific purpose and your specific audience. Here are a few guidelines to help you make the right decision.

1. In an informative speech, state your thesis early, clearly, and directly.
2. In a persuasive speech given to a neutral audience, state your thesis explicitly and early in your speech.
3. In a persuasive speech given to an audience in favor of your position, you may leave the thesis unstated or may state it late in the speech.
4. In a persuasive speech to an audience hostile to your position, delay stating your thesis until you have moved your listeners closer to your position.

Wording the Thesis
State your thesis as a simple declarative sentence. This will help you focus your thinking, your collection of materials, and your organizational pattern (as already noted). You may, however, phrase your thesis in a number of different ways when you present it to your audience. At one extreme, you may state it to your audience as you phrased it for yourself. Here are a few examples:

- We should support Wainwright.
- My thesis is that we should support Wainwright.
- I want to tell you in this brief speech why we should support Wainwright.

Or, you may decide to state your thesis as a question, for example:

- Why should we support Wainwright?
- Are there valid reasons for supporting Wainwright? I think so.
- What are the two main theories of jealousy?

In persuasive speeches in which you face a hostile or mildly opposed audience, you may wish to state your thesis in vague and ambiguous terms. Here are some examples:

- I want to talk about Wainwright's qualifications.
- Does Wainwright deserve our support? Let's look at the evidence.

In these cases you focus the audience's attention on your central idea, but you delay presenting your specific point of view until a more favorable time.

A Note on Thesis and Purpose

The thesis and the purpose are similar in that they both guide you in selecting and organizing your materials. In some ways, however, they are different.

Thesis and purpose differ in their form of expression. The thesis is phrased as a complete declarative sentence. The purpose is phrased as an infinitive phrase (to inform, to persuade).

A more important difference is that the thesis is message-oriented; the purpose is audience-oriented. The thesis identifies the central idea of your speech; it summarizes and epitomizes the speech content. The purpose identifies the change you hope to achieve in your audience, for example, to gain information or to change attitudes.

Another distinguishing factor is that the thesis is usually stated somewhere in the speech. Often, for example, the speaker will state the thesis in the introduction or perhaps as a preface to the main ideas. The purpose, however, is rarely stated. You would rarely say, for example, "I want to persuade you to vote for me" or "I'm going to convince you to buy Brand X." However, you might say (in thesis form), "I'm the most qualified candidate" or "Brand X is an excellent product."

Here are a few more examples to clarify further the difference between thesis and purpose:

Thesis: We can reduce our phone bills by following three rules.

Purpose: To inform my audience of three ways to save on their phone bills.

Thesis: Computer science knowledge is essential for all students.

Purpose: To persuade my audience to take a computer science course.

Especially in these early stages of mastering public speaking, formulate both the thesis statement and the purpose. With both the thesis and the purpose clearly formulated, you should avoid giving a speech that rambles and that audiences find difficult to understand and remember.

YOUR MAJOR PROPOSITIONS

Once your thesis is clearly stated, you can use it to identify your major propositions— that is, your principal assertions or main points. If your speech were a play, the propositions would be its acts. Let's consider how to select and word these propositions and how they may be related to each other.

Selecting and Wording Propositions

In discussing the thesis, we mentioned how you can develop your main points or propositions by asking strategic questions. To see how this works in more detail, imagine that you are giving a speech to a group of high school students on the values of a college education. Your thesis is, "A college education is valuable." You then ask, "Why is it valuable?" From this question you generate your major propositions. Your first step might be to brainstorm this question and generate as many answers as possible without evaluating them. You may come up with answers such as the following:

1. It helps you get a good job.
2. It increases your earning potential.
3. It gives you greater job mobility.
4. It helps you secure more creative work.
5. It helps you to appreciate the arts more fully.
6. It helps you to understand an extremely complex world.
7. It helps you understand different cultures.
8. It allows you to avoid taking a regular job for a few years.
9. It helps you meet lots of people and make new friends.
10. It helps you increase your personal effectiveness.

Of course, we could go on, but for purposes of illustration, we have 10 possible main points. But not all 10 are equally valuable or relevant to your audience. And so you would look over the list and see what you can do to make it shorter and more meaningful. Try these suggestions:

1. Eliminate Those Points That Seem Least Important to Your Thesis
On this basis you might want to eliminate number 8 as it seems least consistent with your intended emphasis on the positive values of college.

2. Combine Those Points That Have a Common Focus   Notice, for example, that the first four points all center on the values of college in terms of jobs. You might, therefore, consider grouping these four items into one proposition: *A college education helps you get a good job.*

This point might be one of your major propositions that could be developed by defining what you mean by a "good job." In the process you might use some of the other ideas you generated in your brainstorming session. This main point or proposition and its elaboration might look like this:

I. A college education helps you get a good job.
   A. College graduates earn higher salaries.
   B. College graduates enter more creative jobs.
   C. College graduates have greater job mobility.

Note that (A), (B), and (C) are all aspects or subdivisions of "a good job."

3. Select Points That Are Most Relevant to or Interest Your Audience
On this basis you might eliminate number 5 and number 7 on the assumption that the audience will not see learning about the arts or different cultures as exciting or valuable at the present time. You might also decide that high school students would be more interested in increasing personal abilities. And so you might select number 10 for inclu-

sion as a second major proposition: *A college education increases your personal effectiveness.*

Earlier you developed the subordinate points in your first proposition—the (A), (B), and (C) of (I) above—by defining more clearly what you meant by a "good job." You would follow the same process here by defining what you mean by "personal effectiveness." It might look something like this:

    I. A college education helps increase your personal effectiveness.
        A. A college education helps you improve your ability to communicate.
        B. A college education helps you acquire the skills for learning how to think.
        C. A college education helps you acquire coping skills.

Follow the same procedure you used to generate the subordinate points (A), (B), and (C) to develop the subheadings under (A), (B), and (C). For example, point (A) might be divided into two major subheads:

        A. A college education helps improve your ability to communicate.
           1. College improves your writing skills.
           2. College improves your speech skills.

You would develop points (B) and (C) in essentially the same way by defining more clearly (in B) what you mean by "learning how to think" and (in C) what you mean by "coping skills."

Some Additional Guidelines

Now that the general process of identifying and developing your main points is understood, here are a few additional guidelines.

1. Use Two, Three, or Four Main Points For your class speeches, which will generally range from 5 to 15 minutes, use two, three, or four main propositions. Too many main points will result in a speech that is confusing, contains too much information and too little amplification, and proves difficult to remember.

2. Develop Your Main Points So They Are Separate and Discrete Do not allow your main points to overlap each other. Each section labeled with a Roman numeral should be a separate entity.

Not This:
    I. Color and style are important in clothing selection.

This:
    I. Color is important in clothing selection.
    II. Style is important in clothing selection.

3. Use the Principle of Balance Devote about equal time to each of your main points. A useful rule of thumb is to give about equal time to each item having the same symbol in your outline. Give each Roman numeral about equal time, each item denoted by a capital letter about the same amount of time, and so on. Break this rule only when you have an especially good reason.

USING SUPPORTING MATERIALS

CHAPTER CONTENTS

Amplifying Materials
   Examples and Illustrations
   Testimony
   Audiovisual Aids

Arguments
   Using Specific Instances and Generalizations
   Using Reasoning from Analogy
   Using Cause-Effect Reasoning
   Using Reasoning from Sign

Motivational Appeals
   Altruism
   Fear
   Individuality and Conformity
   Power, Control, and Influence
   Self-esteem and Approval
   Love and Affiliation
   Achievement
   Financial Gain
   Status
   Self-actualization

Credibility
   Competence
   Character
   Charisma

CHAPTER GOALS

After completing this chapter, you should be able to

1. use examples and illustrations, testimony, and audiovisual aids to amplify your ideas

2. use arguments from specific instances, analogy, causes and effects, and sign effectively

3. use a variety of motivational appeals in your speeches

4. communicate credibility by establishing your competence, character, and charisma

---

Once you have identified your specific purpose and your main assertions, devote your attention to supporting or amplifying them. In this chapter we explain a variety of ways to support your assertions: amplifying materials, arguments and evidence, motivational appeals, and credibility appeals.

AMPLIFYING MATERIALS

Amplifying materials make your assertions clear and vivid, and may help to prove the truthfulness or the validity of your assertions. Examples and illustrations, testimony, and audiovisual aids are the most important forms of amplification. Another form of amplification, definitions, is discussed in Chapter 11 on the informative speech.

Examples and Illustrations

A relatively brief specific instance is referred to as an *example*. A longer and more detailed example told in narrative or storylike form is referred to as an *illustration*.

Examples and illustrations are useful when you wish to make an abstract concept or idea concrete. For example, it is difficult for the audience to see exactly what you mean by such abstract concepts as "persecution," "denial of freedom," or "friendship" unless you provide specific examples and illustrations of what you mean.

To talk in general terms about starvation in various parts of the world might have some effect on the listeners. But one example or illustration of a 6-year-old girl who roams the streets eating garbage makes the idea of starvation vivid and real. In a speech on lead poisoning, Brenda Dempsey (Boaz & Brey, 1988), a student from Eastern Michigan University, used a specific example to stress the importance of her topic:

> When Denise Waddle and her family moved to a nice, middle-class section of Jersey City, New Jersey, they had dreams of healthy living, block parties, even a big back yard so their kid could make mud pies. In less than one year in their new home, their two year old son had been poisoned, and their newborn showed high levels of poisoning in his bloodstream. Unknowingly, the Waddles had been poisoned by their own back yard, for high levels of lead contaminated their water, and their lives.

Using Examples and Illustrations   Examples and illustrations are useful for explaining a concept; they are not ends in themselves. Make them only as long as necessary to ensure that your purpose is achieved. At the same time, make sure that the examples are sufficient to re-create your meaning in the minds of your listeners.

Make the relationship between your assertion and your example explicit. Remember that this relationship is clear to you because you have constructed the speech. The audience is going to hear your speech only once, so the relevance of your example must be clear. Consider the following excerpt in which Stella Guerra (1986) uses a series of examples to illustrate the progress made by women in government and the military. Notice how much more effective these examples are than if she had simply said, "Women have made great progress in government and in the military."

> In short, we are continuing to help America forge an environment that says—opportunities are abundant.
>
> In this environment of prosperity we've seen many *firsts*:
> The first female brigadier general
> The first female astronaut
> The first female sky marshall
> The first female ambassador to the United Nations
> The first female justice of the Supreme Court
> The first female director of Civil Service
> The first female U.S. Customs rep in a foreign country
> The first female to graduate at the very top of the class in a service academy—Navy '84; Air Force '86
> The list goes on and on—and this same progress can be seen in all sectors of our society.

Testimony

Testimony—either the opinions of experts or the accounts of witnesses—helps to amplify your assertions by adding a note of authority to your arguments. For example, you might state an economist's predictions concerning inflation and depression. Or you might cite the testimony of someone who saw an accident, a person who spent two years in a maximum-security prison, or a person who had a particular operation.

Testimony is also of value when you wish to persuade an audience. For example, you might cite an education professor's opinion about the problems confronting education in an effort to persuade your listeners that certain changes must be made in our schools.

Using Testimony   When you cite testimony, stress the competence of the person, whether that person is an expert or a witness. To cite the predictions of a world-famous economist whom your audience has never heard of will mean little unless you first explain the person's competence. For example:

> This prediction emanates from the world's leading economist, who has successfully predicted all major financial trends over the past 20 years.

Second, stress the unbiased nature of the testimony. If the audience perceives the testimony to be biased—whether or not it really is—it will have little effect.

Third, stress the recency of the statement to the audience. Recency is often a crucial factor in determining whether or not listeners will believe a statement.

Fourth, it is usually better to present the testimony of another in your own words, unless of course the quotation is short, comprehensible to the audience, and related directly to the point you are trying to make. If it isn't, paraphrase the ideas. Do note, of course, that the ideas are borrowed from your authority or source.

Audiovisual Aids

When you are planning to give a speech, give some consideration to using some kind of visual or auditory aid. AV aids are not an added frill. They are integral parts of your speech and serve important functions, such as

- gaining attention and maintaining interest
- adding clarity
- aiding audience memory
- reinforcing what you say

Types of Audiovisual Aids   Here are a few types of audiovisuals that you might consider using in your speech.

- As a general rule (to which there are many exceptions), the best audiovisual aid is the *object* itself; bring it to your speech if you can.
- *Models*—replicas of the actual object—help clarify the size of various structures, their position, and how they interface with each other.
- Use the *chalkboard* to record key terms or important definitions or even to outline your speech, but be careful not to talk to the board.
- *Transparent and opaque projections* are useful for key terms or outlines that are complex and that you want your listeners to see as well as hear.
- *Handouts* are useful for presenting complex information that you want your audience to refer to throughout your speech. Use the handout only when it is essential; you don't want to have to remind your listeners to ignore the handout and concentrate on what you're saying.
- Simple *word charts* help you highlight the major points you wish to cover in your speech. For example, in a speech on "how to read a book" the word chart presented in Figure 6.1 clearly identifies the major steps the speaker is discussing. Such charts may be used with the introduction's orientation, with the major points in the body, or with the conclusion's summary. The *organizational chart*, as in Figure 18.1 in *Human Communication*, shows how an organization is structured and the relationships among individuals. The **flip chart**, a pad of paper of about 24 inches square, is mounted on a stand. As you deliver your speech, you flip the pages of the pad to reveal the visuals you want your audience to see.
- Use *graphs* for showing differences over time, for showing how a whole is divided into parts, and for showing different amounts or sizes. The *bar graph* in Figure 6.2 illustrates the changes taking place in college majors. Use a *pie graph* (*pie chart*) to show how some whole is divided into its parts (see Figure 5.2 in *Human Communication*). *Line charts* are useful when you want

How to Read a Book
1. Preview
2. Read for Understanding
3. Read for Retention
4. Review

FIGURE 6.1 A word chart.

to show changes or trends over a particular time period. Figure 6.3, for example, illustrates the sales for a small grocery store over the last six years and shows how rapidly the business has grown.

- Use *maps* for showing geographic elements as well as changes throughout history, population density, immigration patterns, economic conditions, the location of various resources, and hundreds of other issues you may wish to develop in your speeches.
- Use *people* to demonstrate the muscles of the body, different voice patterns, skin complexions, or hairstyles. People as aids also help to secure and maintain the attention and interest of the audience.
- Use *slides* to show various scenes or graphics that you cannot describe in words. The great advantages of slides are their attention-getting value and their ease of preparation and use.
- If the *picture or illustration* is large enough for all members of the audience to see clearly (say, poster size), if it clearly shows what you want to illustrate, and if it is mounted on cardboard, then it will prove useful in your speech. Otherwise, it may cause more problems than it solves.
- *Records and tapes* can be useful for many types of speeches. For example, a

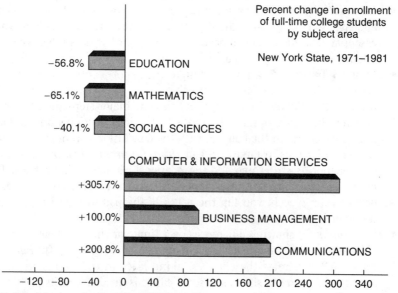

FIGURE 6.2 A bar graph. (*Source:* "1985 Facts & Figures for New York State Public Schools," NYS School Boards Association.)

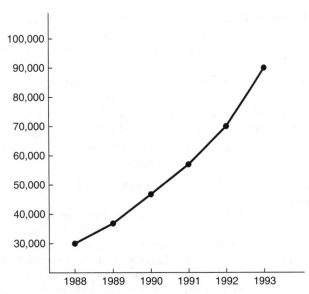

FIGURE 6.3 A line chart.

speech on advertising would be greatly helped by having actual samples of advertising as played on radio or television.

Using Audiovisual Aids Use the aid when you want the audience to concentrate on it—when it will reinforce the message—and then remove it. If the aid remains visible while you have moved on to the next topic, it becomes a distraction or noise. If you are using the chalkboard, write the terms or draw the diagrams when you want the audience to see them and then erase them.

When planning to use audiovisual aids, know them intimately. Be sure you know what order they are to be used in and what you will say when you introduce them. Know exactly what goes where and when.

Test the audiovisual aids prior to your speech. Be certain that they can be easily seen from all parts of the room. If you are using an audio aid, make sure *your* equipment works.

Rehearse your speech with the audiovisual aids incorporated into the presentation. Practice the actual movements with the actual aids you will use. If you are going to use a chart, how will you use it? Will it stand by itself? Will you tape it to the board (and do you have tape with you)? Will you ask another student to hold it for you? Will you hold it yourself?

Avoid the common mistake that many speakers make when using audiovisuals and that is to talk to the aid instead of the audience. Both you and the aid should be focused on the audience. Talk to your audience at all times. Know your aids so well that you can point to what you want without breaking eye contact with your audience.

ARGUMENTS

Here are some suggestions and examples for presenting your arguments and evidence to your audience.

Using Specific Instances and Generalizations

In reasoning from specific instances to general principles, stress that your specific instances are sufficient in number to warrant the conclusion you are drawing, that the specific instances are in fact representative of the whole, that your sample was not drawn disproportionately from one subgroup, and that there was an absence of significant exceptions. That is, you will be more convincing if you answer the questions that an intelligent and critical listener will ask of your evidence.

Carole Howard (1984), in a speech delivered at the 75th Anniversary Conference of Women in Communication, effectively uses numerous specific instances (only some of which are included here) to support her thesis:

> Join me, if you would, on a random walk through the pages of the business press over the last few months:
>
> *The New York Times* on July 5 published an article that said putting a woman on your board is no longer in vogue, so progress has gotten slower. Today women fill only about 3 percent of the 14,000 directorships covered by the Fortune 1000 companies.
>
> *The Wall Street Journal* on July 16 carried an article on research about men's views on women as bosses. The fact that there are enough women bosses to warrant a study is *good* news. The fact that it's news at *all* says we've a ways to go.
>
> *Fortune* magazine published a cover story in the August 20 issue on corporate spouses. The good news is that they kissed the so-called traditional corporate wife goodbye and used the word *spouse*. The bad news is that the only examples of women executives were in a sidebar, literally and figuratively set apart from the main story describing male CEOs and their wives.

Using Reasoning from Analogy

When drawing an analogy, stress the numerous and significant similarities between the items being compared and minimize the differences between them. Mention differences that do exist and that the audience will think of, but show that these do not destroy the validity of your argument. If the audience knows that there are differences, but you do not confront these differences squarely, your argument is going to prove ineffective. The listeners will be wondering, "But what about the difference in . . . ?"

Here, for example, Tom Doyle (Boaz & Brey, 1987) uses a figurative analogy to argue against the usefulness of tariffs against Japanese products:

> The Reagan administration responded to recent trade problems with the Japanese by announcing a policy of limited protectionism, where tariffs are slapped upon Japanese electronic chips, the equivalent of bonking your friend over the head with a pool cue when he beats you at the game.

As this example illustrates, the figurative analogy only creates an image. It does not prove anything. Its main purpose is to clarify, and it is particularly useful when you wish to make a complex process or relationship clearly understandable to the audience.

Using Cause-Effect Reasoning

To use this technique effectively, stress the causal connection by pointing out that other causes are not significant and may for all practical purposes be ruled out. Also note that the causal connection is in the direction postulated, that the cause is indeed the cause and the effect is the effect. Similarly, emphasize that the evidence points to a causal connection—that the relationship is not merely related in time.

Here Richard Snyder (1984) uses reasoning from cause to effect but without offering any real evidence of the connection linking assumed cause and assumed effect:

> We have been through two tumultuous decades: The '60s and the '70s, in which the liberals dominated the media and the trends. What happened—*Education lagged badly.* Look at the SAT scores. Look at illiteracy, absenteeism, crime in city schools. How do you study with the TV turned on? Higher education is currently under fire for mushy curricula and poor scholarship. Compare us to foreigners. We suffer.
>
> *Family life* came apart in many ways. Employed wives are part of the explanation, but it is difficult not to associate the trends with TV viewing. TV cannot tell us that its commercials have big appeal to consumers and at the same time disavow any connection between violent programs and the wife abuse, child abuse, shootings, stabbings, batteries, and the overall upsurge in crime.

Using Reasoning from Sign

As is true with cause-effect reasoning, stress the certainty of the connection between the sign and the conclusion. Make the audience see that because these signs are present, no other conclusion is likely. Make the connection between the signs and the conclusions clear to the audience. You the speaker may know of the connection between enlarged eyes and hyperthyroidism, but this does not mean the audience knows it. State explicitly that enlarged eyes can only be produced by hyperthyroidism and that, therefore, the sign (enlarged eyes) can lead to only one reasonable conclusion (hyperthyroidism).

MOTIVATIONAL APPEALS

In using motivational appeals, you can address many specific motives. Naturally each audience will be a bit different, and motives that are appropriately appealed to in one situation might be inappropriate or ineffective in another. You will always have to exercise judgment and taste.

Altruism

Appeals to altruism are most effective when done with moderation. If they are not moderate, they will seem unrealistic and out of touch with the way real people think in a world that is practical and difficult to survive in.

Here is an especially good example of the use of the appeal to altruism. In this speech Charlotte Lunsford (1988) appeals to altruism but also to a wide variety of other motives. She effectively uses the principle that appeals to a wide variety of motives work best:

> Volunteerism still combines the best and the most powerful values in our society—pride in the dignity of work, the opportunity to get involved in things that affect us, the freedom of choice and expression, the chance to put into practice an ethic of caring, and the realization that one person can make a difference.
>
> To these altruistic reasons for volunteering, we can add some very specific rewards for giving of one's time in the service of others:

- A chance to do the things that one does best.
- Working with a respected community organization.

- Seeing the results of one's own work.
- The opportunity to make business and professional contacts—"networking."
- The opportunity to develop social skills.
- And the chance to move to paid employment.

Fear

The use of fear in persuasion has been studied extensively, and the results show that strong amounts of fear work best (Allen & Preiss, 1990; Boster & Mongeau, 1984). With low or even moderate levels of fear, the audience is not motivated sufficiently to act. With high levels of fear they perk up and begin to listen.

In this excerpt Michael Marien (1984) appeals to fear in his speech on the need to control our modern technologies:

> And the bad news is awesome. There are some 50,000 to 60,000 nuclear warheads in the world today, with a total explosive yield of 1.6 million times that of the 1945 Hiroshima bomb that we use as a benchmark. A single 20-megaton bomb, which could be dropped on New York City, has 1600 times the yield of the Hiroshima bomb. Our modern arsenal amounts to 5000 times the destructive power of all munitions used in World War II. So we do indeed have the potential to end all life on our planet, as a group of scientists recently warned in sketching a scenario of a possible nuclear winter.

Individuality and Conformity

Successful motivation depends on your making your listeners see themselves as standing out from the crowd but never as "outsiders." Make your listeners see themselves as individuals who have a unique identification but who are nevertheless closely identified with the positively evaluated groups. Inspirational speeches use this appeal often:

> You are the ones who will lead the next generation. . . .

> As college students you have a responsibility to contribute your talents to your community. . . .

Power, Control, and Influence

You will motivate your listeners when you enable them to believe that they can increase their power, control, and influence as a result of their learning what you have to say or doing as you suggest. When you tell your audience how they can gain control over their time, become more influential, sell more cars, or teach more effectively, you are giving your audience the tools of power, control, and influence and will have an attentive and positive audience.

Self-esteem and Approval

Show your audience how they can be more self-confident, how they can see themselves as worthy and contributing human beings and you will have an attentive audience. Inspirational speeches, speeches of the "you are the greatest" type, never seem to lack receptive and suggestive audiences.

Show your listeners that by accepting your propositions, they will achieve approval from others. Such approval will also ensure their attaining a number of related goals. For example, if they have peer approval, they will also have influence. If they have approval, they will likely have status. In relating your propositions to your audience's desire for approval, avoid being too obvious. Few people want to be told that they need or desire approval.

Love and Affiliation

If you can tell your audience how to be loved and how to love, or how to have friends and be popular, you will have not only an attentive but also a grateful audience.

In this excerpt Leo Buscaglia (1988), noted author and lecturer, appeals to our desire for love and affiliation:

> It is not uncommon these days to form relationships based on nothing more than mutual physical attraction. On this shaky foundation we set high standards and impossible expectations. We insist that the "magic" continue, that the honeymoon last forever. We resist the reality that love can also mean carrying out the trash, meeting car payments, standing in line at the grocery store and doing the laundry. Relationships that are based on little more than a steamy attraction more often than not end by leaving us bewildered, wondering what went wrong when we find that we are no longer "happily-ever-after." We usually discover that it was the small conflicts, the petty peeves, the infantile rigidity and stubbornness, the disillusionment and the refusal to forgive.
>
> There is no simple formula for making us better lovers. At best we can base our love on certain tried-and-true rules that can make a positive beginning.

Achievement

In using the achievement motive, be explicit in stating how your speech, ideas, and recommendations will contribute to the listeners' achievements. If you tell the listeners how they can learn to increase their potential, earn better grades, secure more prestigious jobs, and become more popular with friends, you will have a highly motivated audience.

In a speech on the values of networking, Peter B. Stark (1985) appeals to the achievement motive of his audience and in the process effectively establishes his credibility:

> Networking is the most powerful success tool to get you where you want to go. To be honest, networking is one of the greatest assets I have ever owned.
>
> At the age of 21, I was the Executive Assistant to the President of a $25 million company. An unadvertised position I had gained through a management consultant I had met in Toastmasters International.
>
> At the age of 23, I was the Director of Marketing for the local Caterpillar Tractor Dealer, a $100 million company. Another unadvertised position I received through a community contact. And, at the age of 25, I had enough contacts to open Photomation West, a printing and advertising firm.

Financial Gain

Concern for lower taxes, for higher salaries, for fringe benefits are all related to the money motive. Show the audience that what you are saying or advocating will make them money and they will listen with considerable interest, much as they read the current get-rich-quick books that are flooding the bookstores.

In a speech designed to motivate the audience to take action against certain proposed budget cuts, Cyril F. Brickfield (1985) appeals to the financial motive of his senior citizen audience:

Congress is now considering freezing Social Security COLA's [cost-of-living adjustments]. Congress is willing to force more than a half million of us into poverty. But the defense budget is exempt from any freeze.

Ladies and gentlemen, let me ask you, is it *fair* that older Americans must lose their inflation protection while the Pentagon doesn't?

Status

Status accounts for a great deal of our behavior and is an especially powerful motive in persuasion. To be effective, link your propositions with your specific audience's desire for status.

In this excerpt Kelly Zmak (Boaz & Brey, 1987), a student from San Jose State University, appeals to the audience's desire for status and success:

You know, as college people we all have something in common. We want to be successful. The levels of our success vary, but to be successful is something that we all strive for. Having an advantage in today's world is something none of us would mind. But having a disadvantage is something that none of us can afford. I would say that there are many of you here today that are not capitalizing on your potential, because you do not own a personal computer. And for those of you who do, listen up. Your computer may not have the power, the capabilities, and the features needed to give the home user, the student, and the business person an advantage in today's world.

Self-actualization

According to Abraham Maslow, the self-actualization motive only influences attitudes and behaviors after all other needs are satisfied. And since these other needs are very rarely all satisfied, the time spent appealing to self-actualization might better be spent on other motives. And yet I suspect that regardless of how satisfied or unsatisfied our other desires are, we all have in some part a desire to self-actualize, to become what we feel we are fit for.

Here, for example, William Jackson (1985) appeals to self-actualization in his speech on happiness in life:

One of the greatest wastes of our national resources is the number of young people who never achieve their potential. If you think you can't you won't. If you think you can, there is an excellent chance you will. The cost of excellence is discipline. The cost of mediocrity is disappointment. Only a mediocre person is always at his best. There should be two goals in your life; one is to get what you want in life, and the other is to enjoy your successes. Only the wisest people achieve the latter.

CREDIBILITY

You will be thought credible if you demonstrate that you are competent, have high moral character, and are dynamic or charismatic. Here are some suggestions for communicating these qualities to your audience.

Competence

Demonstrate your competence, your knowledge, your expertise, your command of your subject. Here are some methods you can use.

Tell Listeners of Your Competence Let the audience know of your special experience or training that qualifies you to speak on this specific topic. If you are speaking on communal living and you have lived on a commune yourself, then include this in your speech. Tell the audience of your unique and personal experiences when these contribute to your credibility. Here, for example, G. J. Tankersley (1984), a businessperson, establishes his knowledge concerning educational issues:

> I've probably had more occasions than many other businessmen to consider these subjects over the years. This is largely because I've spent a good part of my own "extracurricular" time on education.
>
> Currently, I'm co-chairman of a drive to raise funds for Auburn University, which is my alma mater. I'm a member of the Business-Higher Education Forum, a group of about 80 business leaders and college presidents who concern themselves with some of the issues I'm going to discuss today. And I've been working at the University of Pittsburgh, where I'm a Vice Chairman of the Board of Trustees and Chairman of the Board of Visitors at the Business School.
>
> Also, I used to teach. Just after World War II and before I started my career in the gas business, I taught thermodynamics for four years at Auburn's Engineering School.

Stress the Competencies of Your Sources If your audience is not aware of them, emphasize the particular competencies of your sources. For example, saying simply, "Senator Smith thinks . . . " does nothing to establish the senator's credibility. Instead, consider saying something like this:

> Senator Smith, who headed the finance committee for three years and was formerly Professor of Economics at MIT, thinks. . . .

In this way it becomes clear to the audience that you have chosen your sources carefully and with a view toward providing the most authoritative sources possible.

Avoid Apologizing Do not needlessly call attention to your inadequacies as a spokesperson or to any gaps in your knowledge. No one can know everything. Your audience does not expect you to be the exception. It is not necessary, however, to remind them of any shortcoming. Stress your competencies, not your inadequacies.

Here is an excerpt from Vice President Dan Quayle's (1988) speech of acceptance of the Republican nomination for vice president of the United States. How effectively does Quayle establish his competence?

> Many this week have asked, who is Dan Quayle? The people of Indiana know me and now the nation will.
>
> Since 1980, I have been a United States Senator from Indiana—and proud of it.
>
> Before that, I was a member of the United States House of Representatives—and proud of.
>
> And, as a young man, I served six years in the National Guard. And, like the millions of Americans who have served in the Guard and who serve today—I am proud of it. In Indiana they call us "Hoosiers" and if you saw the movie *Hoosiers* you have a feeling for what life is like in the small towns of our state.
>
> My hometown of Huntington is a little bigger than the town in the movie, and the high school I graduated from was a little bigger than the one that fielded the basketball

team in the film. Still, I identify with that movie, *Hoosiers*, because it reflects the values I grew up with in our small town. We believe very strongly in hard work, in getting an education, and in offering an opportunity to our families. We love basketball, we love underdogs, but most important, we love our country.

Character

As a speaker, demonstrate those qualities of character that will increase your credibility. Here are some suggestions for demonstrating character.

Stress Fairness   If delivering a persuasive speech, stress that you have examined both sides of the issue (if, indeed, you have). If you are presenting both sides, then make it clear that your presentation is an accurate and fair one. Be particularly careful not to omit any argument the audience may already have thought of; such an omission is a sure sign that your presentation is not a fair and balanced one. Tell the audience that you would not advocate a position if you did not base it on a fair evaluation of the issues.

Stress Concern for Enduring Values   We view speakers who are concerned with small and insignificant issues as less credible than speakers who demonstrate a concern for lasting truths and general principles. Thus, make it clear to the audience that your position—your thesis—is related to higher-order values. Show them exactly how this is true.

Notice how President George Bush (1988) stresses his concern for such enduring values as family, religion, tradition, and individual power in his speech accepting the Republican nomination:

> At the bright center is the individual. And radiating out from him or her is the family, the essential unit of closeness and of love. For it is the family that communicates to our children—to the 21st century—our culture, our religious faith, our traditions and history.
>
> From the individual to the family to the community, and so out to the town, to the church and school and, still echoing out, to the country, the state, the nation—each doing only what it does well, and no more. And I believe that power must always be kept close to the individual, close to the hands that raise the family and run the home.

Stress Concern for Audience   Make it clear to the audience that you are interested in their welfare rather than seeking self-gain. If the audience feels that you are "out for yourself," they will justifiably downgrade your credibility. Make it clear that the audience's interests are foremost in your mind.

Here is an excerpt from Richard Nixon's "Checkers Speech." How effectively does Nixon establish his character?

> Then, in 1942, I went into the service. Let me say that my service record was not a particularly unusual one. I went to the South Pacific. I guess I'm entitled to a couple of battle stars. I got a couple of letters of commendation.
>
> But I was just there when the bombs were falling. And then I returned to the United States, and in 1946 I ran for Congress.
>
> When we came out of the war, Pat and I—Pat during the war had worked as a stenographer, and in a bank, and as an economist for a government agency and when we

came out, the total of our savings, from both my law practice, her teaching, and all the time I was in the war, the total for that entire period was just a little less than $10,000— every cent of that, incidentally, was in government bonds— well, that's where we start, when I got into politics.

Charisma

Demonstrate your charisma by appearing friendly and pleasant rather than aloof and reserved, dynamic rather than hesitant, outspoken and forceful rather than introverted or soft-spoken.

Demonstrate a Positive Outlook   Show the audience that you have a positive orientation to the public-speaking situation and to the entire speaker-audience encounter. Listeners see positive and forward-looking people as more credible than negative and backward-looking people. Stress your pleasure at addressing the audience. Stress hope rather than despair. Stress happiness rather than sadness.

Act Assertively   Show the audience that you are a person who will stand up for your rights. Show them that you will not back off simply because the odds may be against you or because you are outnumbered.

Demonstrate Enthusiasm   The lethargic speaker who plods through the speech is the very opposite of the charismatic speaker. Try viewing a film of Martin Luther King, Jr., or Billy Graham speaking. They are totally absorbed with the speech and with the audience. They are excellent examples of the enthusiasm that makes speakers charismatic.

Although it is difficult to evaluate charisma without hearing the speaker's voice and seeing the speaker's gestures, focus on those aspects that you can identify from just the written word in the following excerpt from Martin Luther King, Jr.'s "I Have a Dream" speech (reprinted in its entirety in *Human Communication,* Unit 21). How effectively does King establish his charisma?

> I say to you today, my friends, so even though we face the difficulties of today and tomorrow, I still have a dream. It is a dream deeply rooted in the American dream.
>
> I have a dream that one day this nation will rise up and live out the true meaning of its creed: "We hold these truths to be self-evident; that all men are created equal."
>
> I have a dream that one day on the red hills of George the sons of former slaves and the sons of former slaveowners will be able to sit down together at the table of brotherhood; I have a dream—
>
> That one day even the state of Mississippi, a state sweltering with the heat of injustice, sweltering with the heat of oppression, will be transformed into an oasis of freedom and justice; I have a dream—
>
> That my four little children will one day live in a nation where they will not be judged by the color of their skin but by the content of their character; I have a dream today.

CHAPTER 7

ORGANIZING YOUR SPEECH

CHAPTER CONTENTS

Thought Patterns
    Topical Pattern
    Problem-Solution Pattern
    Temporal Pattern
    Spatial Pattern
    Cause-Effect/Effect-Cause Pattern
    The Motivated Sequence
    Additional Thought Patterns

Outlining Your Speech
    Constructing the Outline
    Some Mechanics of Outlining
    The Delivery Outline

CHAPTER GOALS

After completing this chapter, you should be able to

1. organize your main assertions into appropriate thought patterns

2. outline your speech effectively

3. prepare a useful delivery outline

Once you have identified the major propositions you wish to include in your speech, devote attention to how you will arrange these propositions in the body of your speech. When you follow a clearly identified organizational pattern, your listeners will be able to see your speech as a whole and will be able to see the connections and relationships among your various pieces of information. Should they have a momentary lapse in attention—as they surely will at some point in just about every speech—they will be able to refocus their attention and not lose your entire train of thought.

THOUGHT PATTERNS

Here we look at the major ways in which you can organize your major propositions in the body of your speech. In Chapter 9 we consider the introduction, conclusion, and transitions.

Topical Pattern

Perhaps the most popular pattern for organizing informative speeches is the topical pattern. When your topic conveniently divides itself into subdivisions, each of which is clear and approximately equal in importance, this pattern is most useful. It is not, however, a catchall category for topics that do not seem to fit into any of the other patterns. Rather, this pattern should be regarded as one appropriate to the particular topic being considered. For example, the topical pattern is an obvious one for organizing a speech on the powers of the government. Here the divisions are clear:

The Powers of Government

    I.   The legislative branch is controlled by Congress.
   II.   The executive branch is controlled by the president.
  III.   The judicial branch is controlled by the courts.

Note that the topic itself, the powers of the government, divides itself into three parts: legislative, executive, and judicial. It remains for you to organize your various materials under these three logical headings.

Problem-Solution Pattern

The problem-solution pattern is especially useful in persuasive speeches, in which you want to convince the audience that a problem exists and that your solution would solve or alleviate the problem.

Try to anticipate any possible objections your listeners might raise and try to answer them along with your discussion of the solution. For example, if you anticipate that your audience will see your solution as too expensive, make sure that you let them know that it will not be too expensive but will, in fact, be quite reasonable.

Let's say you are trying to persuade your audience that teachers should be given higher salaries and increased benefits. Here a problem-solution pattern might be appropriate. You might discuss in the first part of the speech the problems confronting contemporary education—such as (1) industry lures away the most highly qualified graduates, (2) many excellent teachers leave the field after two or three years, and (3) teaching is currently a low-status occupation.

In the second part of your speech you might consider the possible solutions that you wish your audience to accept. These might include the following: (1) salaries for teachers must be made competitive with salaries offered by private industry and (2) the benefits teachers receive must be made as attractive as those offered by industry.

A problem-solution pattern would also be appropriate for a persuasive speech arguing against nuclear plants. Here you would wish to convince your audience that nuclear plants create problems and that we therefore must eliminate them in order to solve the problems. Your speech, "No More Nukes," might look something like this:

I.   Nuclear plants create too many problems.
   A.   Leaks could endanger the lives of workers and the community.
   B.   Nuclear plants endanger the environment.
   C.   A meltdown could occur.

II. The solutions are simple and practical.
   A.   Stop building nuclear plants.
   B.   Dismantle existing nuclear plants.
   C.   Devote resources to the development of alternative energy sources.

Temporal Pattern

The temporal or chronological pattern is especially appropriate for informative speeches, in which you want to describe events or processes that occur over time. A speech on the development of language in the child might be organized in a temporal pattern and could be divided something like this:

The Development of Language

I.   Babbling occurs around the fifth month.
II. Lallation occurs around the sixth month.
III. Echolalia occurs around the ninth month.
IV. "Communication" occurs around the twelfth month.

Here you would cover each of the events in a time sequence beginning with the earliest stage and working up to the final stage—in this case the stage of true communication.

Spatial Pattern

When you wish to describe objects or places, a spatial pattern is often useful. For example, let's say you want to give a speech on touring Central America. The main headings of such a speech might look something like this:

I.   Your first stop is Cuba.
II. Your second stop is Jamaica.
III. Your third stop is Hispaniola (Haiti and the Dominican Republic).
IV. Your fourth stop is Puerto Rico.

Cause-Effect/Effect-Cause Pattern

If you want to convince your listeners of the causal connection that exists between two events or two elements, then you might try using a cause-effect pattern. For example, a speech on hypertension, designed to spell out some of the causes and effects, might look like this:

    I.   There are three main causes of hypertension.
        A. High salt intake increases blood pressure.
        B. Excess weight increases blood pressure.
        C. Anxiety increases blood pressure.

   II.   There are three major effects of hypertension.
        A. Nervousness increases.
        B. Heart rate increases.
        C. Shortness of breath increases.

The Motivated Sequence

The motivated sequence consists of five steps—attention, need, satisfaction, visualization, and action—and is useful for both persuasive and informative speeches (Gronbeck, McKerrow, Ehninger, & Monroe, 1992).

Attention   Your first step is to gain attention and focus it on your topic. If you execute this step effectively, your audience should be anxious and ready to hear what you have to say. You can gain audience attention through a variety of means (see Chapter 9).

Need   Second, demonstrate that a need exists. Make the audience realize that something has to be learned or something has to be done. This need may be established in four parts:

   1. State the need or problem as it exists or will exist.
   2. Illustrate the need with specific examples.
   3. Further support the existence of the need with additional illustrations, testimony, and the other forms of support identified in Chapter 6.
   4. Show how this need affects your specific listeners, for example, how it affects their financial status, their career goals, or their individual happiness.

Satisfaction   Present the "answer" or the "solution" to satisfying the need that you demonstrated above. If you do this effectively, your audience should agree that what you are informing them about or persuading them to do will effectively satisfy the need. This satisfaction step usually involves:

   1. a statement (with examples and illustrations if necessary) of what you want the audience to learn, believe, or do
   2. a statement of how or why what you are asking them to learn, believe, or do will lead to satisfying the need identified in Step 2

Visualization   Next you intensify the audience's feelings or beliefs. Take the audience beyond the present time and place and help them to imagine the situation as it would be if the need were satisfied as you suggest. There are two basic ways of doing this:

1. Demonstrate the benefits that the audience would get if your ideas were put into operation.
2. Demonstrate the negative effects that the audience would suffer if your plan were not put into operation.

Of course, you could combine these two methods and demonstrate both the benefits of your plan and the negative consequences of the existing plan or of some alternative plan.

Action   Your last step is to tell the audience what they should do to ensure that the need (as demonstrated in Step 2) is satisfied (as stated in Step 3). That is, show them what they must do to satisfy the need. Move the audience in a particular direction—to speak in favor of additional research funding for AIDS or against cigarette advertising, to attend the next student government meeting, to contribute free time to read for the blind, and so on. You can accomplish this step by stating exactly what the audience members should do, using an emotional appeal, or giving the audience guidelines for future action.

Here is a much abbreviated example of how these five steps would look in a speech designed to inform an audience about the workings of home computers.

> [Introduction]
> *Attention*
> By the time we graduate, there will be more home computers than automobiles. [You might then go on to explain the phenomenal growth of computers in education until you have the complete attention of your audience revolving around the importance and growth of computers.]
> [Body]
> *Need*
> Much as it is now impossible to get around without a car, it will be impossible to get around the enormous amount of information without a home computer. [You might then go on to explain how knowledge is expanding so rapidly that it will be extremely difficult to keep up with any field without computer technology.]
> *Satisfaction*
> Learning a few basic principles of home computers will enable us to process our work more efficiently, in less time, and more enjoyably. [You might explain the various steps that your listeners could take to satisfy the needs you already identified.]
> *Visualization*
> With these basic principles firmly in mind (and a home computer), you'll be able to stay at home and do your library research for your next speech by just punching in the correct code. [You might then go through in more or less detail the speech research process so that your listeners will be able to visualize exactly what the advantages of computer research will be.]
> [Conclusion]
> *Action*
> These few principles should be supplemented by further study. Probably the best way to further your study is to enroll in a computer course. Another useful way is to read the brief paperback, *The Home Computer for the College Student.* [You could identify the several computer courses that are available and that would be appropriate for a beginning student. Further, you might identify a few other books or perhaps distribute a brief list of books that would be appropriate reading for the beginning student.]

In an informative speech you could have stopped after the satisfaction step because you would have accomplished your goal of informing the audience about some principles of home computers. But in some cases you may feel it helpful to complete the steps to emphasize your point in detail. In a persuasive speech, you must go at least as far as visualization (if your purpose is limited to strengthening or changing attitudes or beliefs) or to the action step (if you aim to motivate behavior).

Additional Thought Patterns

The six thought patterns just considered are the most common and the most useful for most public speeches. But there are other patterns that might be appropriate for different topics. Here are several such patterns.

- The *structure-function pattern* is useful in informative speeches in which you want to discuss how something is constructed (its structural aspects) and what it does (its functional aspects).
- Arranging your material in a *comparison-and-contrast pattern* is useful in informative speeches in which you want to analyze two different theories, proposals, departments, or products in terms of their similarities and differences.
- The *pro-and-con pattern*, sometimes called the advantages-disadvantages pattern, is useful in informative speeches in which you want to explain objectively the advantages (the pros) and the disadvantages (the cons) of each plan, method, or product.
- The *claim and proof pattern* is especially useful in a persuasive speech in which you want to prove the truth or usefulness of a particular proposition. In this pattern your speech would consist of two major parts. In the first part you would explain your claim (tuition must not be raised, library hours must be expanded). In the second part you would offer your evidence or proof as to why tuition must not be raised, for example.
- The *multiple definition pattern* is useful for informative speeches in which you want to explain the nature of a concept (what is a born-again Christian? what is a scholar? what is multiculturalism?). In this pattern each major heading would consist of a different type of definition or way of looking at the concept. A variety of definition types are discussed in Chapter 11.
- The *Who-What-Why-Where-When* pattern is the pattern of the journalist and is useful in informative speeches when you wish to report or explain an event like a robbery, political coup, war, or trial. Here each major part of your speech would answer one of these questions.

OUTLINING YOUR SPEECH

The outline is a blueprint for your speech; it lays out the elements of the speech and their relationship to each other. With this blueprint in front of you, you can see at a glance all the elements of your speech as you will communicate them to your audience. And, like a blueprint for a building, the outline helps you spot weaknesses that might otherwise go undetected.

Begin outlining at the time you begin constructing your speech. Do not wait until you have collected all your material, but begin outlining as you are collecting material, organizing it, and styling it. In this way you will be able to take best advantage of one of the major functions of outlines—to tell you where change is needed. The outline should be changed and altered as necessary at every stage of the speech construction process.

Outlines may be extremely detailed or extremely general. In fact, the entire speech may be arranged in outline form, that is, with every item of information arranged not in paragraph form (as it might be in speaking from manuscript), but in outline form. At the other extreme, an outline may consist of key terms listed in the order you'll cover them.

The more detail you put into the outline, the easier it will be to examine the parts of the speech for all the qualities and characteristics that were discussed in the previous chapters. Consequently, it is a good idea, at least in the beginning, to outline your speeches in detail and in complete sentences. The usefulness of an instructor's criticism will often depend on the completeness of the outline.

Constructing the Outline

After you have completed your research and have an organizational plan for your speech mapped out, put this blueprint—this outline—on paper, using the following guidelines.

Preface the Outline with Identifying Data   Before you begin the outline proper, identify the general and specific purposes as well as your thesis. This prefatory material should look something like this:

General purpose: to inform
Specific purpose: to inform my audience of four major functions of the mass media
Thesis: the mass media serve four major functions

These identifying notes are not part of your speech proper. They are not mentioned in your oral presentation. Rather, they are guides to the preparation of the speech and the outline. They are like road signs to keep you going in the right direction and to signal when you have gone off course. One additional bit of identifying data should preface the introduction: the title of your speech.

Outline the Introduction, Body, and Conclusion as Separate Units
Each of these three parts of the speech, although intimately connected, should be labeled separately and should be kept distinct in your outline. Like the identifying data above, these labels are not spoken to the audience but rather are further guides to your preparation.

Insert Transitions and Internal Summaries   Using square brackets [ ], insert transitions (discussed in depth in Chapter 9) between the introduction and the body, the body and the conclusion, the major propositions of the body, and wherever else you think they might be useful. Insert your internal summaries (if these are not integrated with your transitions) wherever you feel they will help your audience to understand and remember your ideas.

Append a List of References   Some instructors require that you append to your speeches a list of references. If this is requested, then do so at the end of the outline or on a separate page.

Whatever the specific requirements, these sources will prove most effective with your audience if you integrate them into the speech. It will count for little if you consulted the latest works by the greatest authorities but never mention this to your audience. When appropriate, weave into your speech the source material you have consulted.

Some Mechanics of Outlining

Assuming that the outline you construct for your early speeches will be relatively complete, here are a few guidelines concerning the mechanics of outlining.

Use a Consistent Set of Symbols   The following is the standard, accepted sequence of symbols for outlining:

    I.
        A.
            1.
                a.
                    (1)
                        (a)

Use Visual Aspects to Reflect the Organizational Pattern   Use proper and clear indentation. This will help to set off visually coordinate and subordinate relationships.

Not This:

    I. Television caters to the lowest possible intelligence.
        A. Situation comedies
            1. "Growing Pains"

This:

    I. Television caters to the lowest possible intelligence.
        A. Situation comedies illustrate this.
            1. "Growing Pains"
            2. "Family Ties"
            3. "Who's the Boss?"
        B. Soap operas illustrate this.
            1. "As the World Turns"
            2. "General Hospital"
            3. "The Young and the Restless"

Use One Discrete Idea Per Symbol   Compound sentences are sure give-aways that you have not limited each item to a single idea. Also, be sure that each item is discrete—that it does not overlap with any other item.

Not This:

I.   Education might be improved if teachers were better trained and if students were better motivated.

This:

I.   Education would be improved if teachers were better trained.
II.   Education would be improved if students were better motivated.

Note that in *This*, items I and II are single ideas but in *Not This* they are combined.

Use Complete Declarative Sentences   Phrase your ideas in the outline in complete declarative sentences rather than as questions or as phrases. This will further assist you in examining the essential relationships. It is much easier, for example, to see if one item of information supports another if both are phrased in the declarative mode. If one is a question and one is a statement, this will be more difficult.

Not This:

I.   Who should raise children?
II.   Should the state raise children?
   A.   Equality for children
   B.   Parents will be released for work.

This:

I.   Children should be raised by the state.
   A.   All children will be treated equally.
   B.   Parents will be released to work.

Note that in *This*, all items are phrased as complete declarative sentences and their relationship is clear. In *Not This*, on the other hand, a mixture of question, sentence, and phrase obscures the important relationships among the items in the outline.

The following outline (Figure 7.1), with side notes explaining its structures and functions, will help clarify the various facets of organization and outlining.

Figure 7.2 (p. 68) presents a skeletal outline that you might find useful in visualizing how your speech should be organized. Naturally, you would have to modify this for your specific purposes. For example, if you had fewer or more than three main points, you would adjust the body of the speech outline accordingly.

The Delivery Outline

Now that you have constructed what is called a preparation outline, you need to construct a delivery outline, an outline that will assist you in delivering the speech. Resist the temptation to use your preparation outline to deliver the speech. If you do, you will tend to read from the outline, which is not a very effective way to give a speech. Instead, construct a brief delivery outline, one that will assist rather than hinder your delivery of the speech. Here are some guidelines in preparing this delivery outline.

Revealing Yourself to Others

Introduction

I. If you want to get to know yourself better, reveal yourself: self-disclosure.

    A. This may sound peculiar, but it is supported by a great deal of scientific research.

    B. Self-disclosure can lead us to feel better about ourselves but can also lead to lots of problems.

    C. Understanding self-disclosure can lead us to make the most effective use of this most important form of communication.

II. I've immersed myself in self-disclosure for the last five years—as student, researcher, and writer—and want to share some insights with you.

III. In order to understand self-disclosure we need to focus on two aspects.

    A. Self-disclosure is a form of communication in which you reveal information about yourself that is normally kept hidden.

    B. Self-disclosure involves both rewards and problems.

[Let me consider first the definition of self-disclosure.]

Body

I. Self-disclosure is a form of communication in which you reveal information about yourself that is normally kept hidden.

    A. Self-disclosure is a type of communication.

        1. Self-disclosure includes overt statements.

            a. An overt confession of infidelity to your lover is self-disclosure.

            b. A letter explaining why you committed a crime is self-disclosure.

        2. Self-disclosure is not noncommunication.

            a. Writing personal thoughts in a diary that no one sees is not self-disclosure.

            b. Talking to ourselves when no one overhears is not self-disclosure.

    B. Self-disclosure involves information about the self not previously known by the listeners.

        1. Telling people something about someone else is not self-disclosure.

            a. Self-disclosure involves the self.

            b. Self-disclosing statements begin with

Here I try to gain attention by stating what appears to be a contradiction. I could have used a specific instance, a humorous story, an interesting quotation, and various other methods discussed in Chapter 7. The introductory statement used here has the added advantage of introducing the topic immediately. In these two brief statements I emphasize the importance of the topic to the audience to ensure their continued attention and interest.

Note that each statement in the outline is a complete sentence. You can easily convert this full-sentence outline into a phrase or word outline.

Here I establish my connection with the topic and answer the inevitable question of the audience: why I am discussing this particular topic? I also establish my credibility.

In this section I explain exactly what I will cover in the speech. For the sake of clarity I state here the two main points that I cover in the body of the speech in the same language. Note also that these points are repeated in the summary in the conclusion. Different language may and often is used. Note, however, that although this repetition is obvious to you reading the speech, it will not necessarily be obvious to the audience. Listeners will not remember the exact wording used, and yet such repetition will help them remember your speech.

I also state here the specific purpose of the speech—"to understand self-disclosure."

Continued on p. 66

FIGURE 7.1 A sample outline with annotations.

2. Telling people what they already know is not self-disclosure.

C. Self-disclosure involves information normally kept hidden.

   1. Self-disclosure does not involve information that we do not actively keep secret.

   2. Self-disclosure involves only information that we work at to keep hidden, that we expend energy in hiding.

[This, then, is what self-disclosure is; now let us focus on what self-disclosure may involve.]

II. Self-disclosure involves both rewards and problems.

A. There are two main rewards of self-disclosure.

   1. First, we get to know ourselves better.

      a. Talking about my fear of snakes led me to understand the reasons for such fears.

      b. Results from studies show that persons who disclose have greater self-awareness than do those who do not self-disclose.

   2. Second, we can deal with our problems better.

      a. Dealing with guilt is a prime example.

      b. Studies conducted by Civikly, Hecht, and me show that personal problems are more easily managed after self-disclosure.

B. There are two major dangers of self-disclosure.

   1. First, self-disclosure may involve personal problems.

      a. The fear of rejection may be more damaging than retaining the secrets.

      b. Self-disclosure may bring to the surface problems that you are not psychologically ready to deal with.

   2. Second, self-disclosure may involve professional problems.

      a. A number of ex-convicts who disclosed their criminal records have been fired.

      b. Persons who were treated by psychiatrists and who revealed this have had their political careers ruined.

[Let me now summarize in brief some of what we now know about self-disclosure.]

The transitions (indicated here in brackets) are stated in rather obvious terms to emphasize their basic structure and function. As explained earlier, with practice you will develop transitional statements with more grace and subtlety.

This is the first major point of the speech, and here I focus on definitional aspects of self-disclosure. The entire definition is presented in (I), and in (A), (B), and (C) each element in the definition is explained in more detail.

Observe how this transition connects what has been discussed with what is to follow.

Notice how this statement clues the listener to expect a two-part division: rewards and problems. Each of these divisions is further broken down to explain the specific rewards and problems that may be derived from self-disclosure.

Note that here, as in (2) and (3), I provide listeners with guide words (first, second, third) to enable them to keep track of where I am. In the actual speech I might make this even clearer by stating something like "The first reward is that we get to know ourselves better" to emphasize that I am talking about the first reward. This may seem like oversimplifying, but for an audience hearing the speech only once, it will prove helpful.

Note again the parallel structure throughout the speech outline. Focus, for example, on Body (II) (A) and (B), or Body (II) (B) (1), (2), and (3), and elsewhere throughout the speech. This parallel structure helps clarify significant relationships for both the speaker and the listener.

Conclusion

I. Self-disclosure is a unique form of communication.

    A. Self-disclosure is a form of communication in which you reveal information about yourself that is normally kept hidden.

    B. Rewards and problems await self-disclosure.

II. Self-disclosure is probably our most significant form of communication.

    A. It can lead to great advantages and great disadvantages.

    B. By better understanding self-disclosure, we may be in a better position to maximize the advantages and to minimize the disadvantages.

III. So, if you want to get to know yourself better, self-disclose.

This transition tells the audience that the conclusion (containing a summary) is next.

Here I provide a summary of the main points in the speech. Notice that these points correspond to the orientation in the Introduction—(III) (A) and (B)—and to the main points in the Body—(I) and (II). Again, the same wording is used to add clarity.

This section serves two purposes. First, I provide a relatively clear-cut ending to the speech. The last sentence, especially, should make it clear that the speech is finished. Second, I recall the significance of the topic and of the speech. Notice that (II) (C) restates the significance of the topic originally provided in the Introduction (I).

Here I provide closure by referring back to the opening lines of the speech.

Be Brief The delivery outline should not stand in the way of your making contact with your audience. Therefore, keep it brief. Use key words that will trigger in your mind the ideas you wish to discuss with your audience.

Be Clear Be sure that you can see the outline while you are speaking. Do not write so small that you will have to squint to read it. On the other hand, do not write so big that you will need reams of paper to deliver a five-minute speech.

Be Delivery Minded This is your outline. You want it to help you deliver your speech most effectively. Therefore, include any guides to delivery you might wish to remember while you are speaking. For example, you might note in the outline when you will use your visual aid and when you will remove it. A simple "Show VA" or "Remove VA" should suffice.

You might also wish to note some speaking cues such as "slow down" when reading a poetry excerpt, or perhaps a place where an extended pause might help.

Figure 7.3 (p. 69) presents a sample outline suitable for delivery. Note the following features of this delivery outline:

Introduction

    I. _____ .

    II. _____ .

    III. _____ .

        A. _____ .

        B. _____ .

        C. _____ .

[_____]

Body

    I. _____ .

        A. _____ .

        B. _____ .

[_____]

    II. _____ .

        A. _____ .

        B. _____ .

[_____]

    III. _____ .

        A. _____ .

        B. _____ .

[_____]

Conclusion

    I. _____ .

        A. _____ .

        B. _____ .

        C. _____ .

    II. _____ .

    III. _____ .

FIGURE 7.2 A skeletal outline.

1. It follows closely the preparation outline. (Compare this outline with that in Figure 7.1.)
2. It is brief enough so that you will be able to use it effectively as you deliver your speech without losing eye contact with the audience. It uses abbrevia-

PAUSE!
LOOK OVER AUDIENCE!

    I.   Get to know self: SD

        A.   Research supports: feel better

        B.   *BUT,* problems too

        C.   Understanding SD: effectiveness

PAUSE—SCAN AUDIENCE

    II.   Immerse self in SD

    III. Understanding SD

WRITE 2 TOPICS ON BOARD

        A.   SD: form of C

        B.   SD: rewards and problems

[Let's examine SD as a form of C]

    I.   SD: form of C

        A.   Type of C

        B.   *NEW* (not *OLD*) information

        C.   Hidden information

[Now that we know what SD is, let's look at some rewards and problems]

    II.   SD: rewards *AND* problems

TAPE REWARDS/PROBLEMS VISUAL AID CHART TO BOARD

        A.   Rewards: know self better & deal with problems

[*BUT,* there are problems too]

        B.   Problems: personal & professional

PAUSE
STEP FORWARD

[Let's review what we now know about SD]

    I.   SD: unique form of C

    II.   SD: most significant form of C

    III. Get to know self: SD

PAUSE!
ASK FOR QUESTIONS

FIGURE 7.3 A sample delivery outline.

tions (SD for self-disclosure; C for communication) and phrases rather than complete sentences.

3. It is detailed enough to include all the essential parts of your speech, including transitions.

4. It contains delivery notes specifically tailored to your own needs—pause suggestions, terms to be emphasized, and guides to using visual aids.

5. It is clearly divided into introduction, body, and conclusion (though to save space, the labels are omitted and lines are used instead) and uses the same numbering system as the preparation outline.

CHAPTER 8

WORDING YOUR SPEECH

CHAPTER CONTENTS

Oral Style

Choosing Words
   Clarity
   Vividness
   Appropriateness
   Personal Style
   Forcefulness/Power

Phrasing Sentences
   Use Short Sentences
   Use Direct Sentences
   Use Active Sentences
   Use Positive Sentences

CHAPTER GOALS

After completing this chapter, you should be able to

1. distinguish between oral and written style and phrase your ideas using oral style

2. word your speech so that it is clear, vivid, appropriate, personal, and forceful

3. phrase your ideas into sentences that are short, direct, active, and positive

You are a successful public speaker when your listeners create in their minds the meanings you want them to create. You are successful when your listeners adopt the attitudes and behaviors you want them to adopt. The language choices you make—for example, the words you select and the sentences you form—will influence greatly the meanings your listeners get and thus how successful you are.

We focus on two topics relating to effective language use. First, we examine the nature of oral style and distinguish it from the style of the written composition or essay. Second, we offer specific suggestions for selecting words and phrasing sentences to make your speech more effective.

ORAL STYLE

Oral style is a quality of spoken language that is clearly differentiated from written language. You do not speak as you write. The words and sentences you use differ depending on whether you are speaking or writing. The major reason for this difference is that you compose speech instantly. You select your words and construct your sentences as you think your thoughts. There is very little time in between the thought and the utterance. When you write, however, you compose your thoughts after considerable reflection. Even then you probably often rewrite and edit as you go along. Because of this, written language has a more formal tone. Spoken language is more informal, more colloquial.

Spoken and written language not only *do* differ, they *should* differ. The main reason spoken and written language should differ is that the listener hears a speech only once. Therefore, speech must be instantly intelligible. The reader can reread an essay or look up an unfamiliar word. The reader can spend as much time as he or she wishes with a written page. The listener, however, must move at the pace you set as the speaker. The reader may reread a sentence or paragraph if there is a temporal attention lapse. The listener doesn't have this option.

Thus, the two forms of communication differ in the way we produce and receive them. These differences lead speakers and writers to compose differently. At the same time, the differences between the way we read and the way we listen demand that speakers and writers employ different principles to guide them in composing messages.

The words you use in speaking and in writing differ from each other in important ways. Generally, spoken language consists of shorter, simpler, and more familiar words than does written language. There is a great deal more qualification in speech than in writing. For example, when speaking you probably make greater use of such expressions as *although*, *however*, *perhaps*, and the like. When writing, however, you probably edit out such expressions.

Spoken language has a greater number of self-reference terms (terms that refer to the speaker himself or herself). In speaking you are more apt to use such terms as *I*, *me*, *our*, *us*, and *you*. Spoken language contains more specific and concrete terms. Written language contains more general and abstract terms.

Spoken language has more terms that include the speaker as part of the observation (for example, *it seems to me that . . .* or *as I see it . . .*). Further, spoken language contains more verbs and adverbs, whereas writing contains more nouns and adjectives.

For the most part, retain this spoken style in your public speeches. The public speech is composed, however, much like a written essay, with considerable thought, deliberation, editing, and restyling. Thus you will need to devote special effort to retaining and polishing your oral style. In the following chapter, we present specific suggestions for achieving this goal.

CHOOSING WORDS

Choose words to achieve clarity, vividness, appropriateness, a personal style, and forcefulness.

Clarity

Clarity in speaking style should be your primary goal. Here are some guidelines to help you make your speech clear.

Be Economical   Don't waste words. Two of the most important ways to achieve economy are to avoid redundancies and to avoid meaningless words. Notice the redundancy in the following expressions:

very unique
at 9 A.M. *in the morning*
we *first* began the discussion
the full *and complete* report
I *myself personally*
blue *in color*
*over*exaggerate
you, *members of the audience*
clearly unambiguous
about *approximately* ten inches *or so*
cash *money*

By cutting out the italicized terms you get rid of unnecessary words. You thus move closer to a more economical and clearer style.

Use Specific Terms and Numbers   Picture these items:

- A bracelet
- A gold bracelet
- A gold bracelet with a diamond clasp
- A braided gold bracelet with a diamond clasp

Notice that as we get more and more specific, we get a clearer and more detailed picture. Be specific. Don't say *dog* when you want your listeners to picture a St. Bernard. Don't say *car* when you want them to picture a white limousine. Don't say *movie* when you want them to think of *Cliffhanger.*

The same is true of numbers. Don't say "earned a good salary" if you mean "earned $90,000 a year." Don't say "taxes will go up" when you mean "taxes will increase 22 percent." Don't say "the defense budget was enormous" when you mean "the defense budget was $17 billion."

Use Guide Phrases   Listening to a public speech is difficult work. Assist your listeners by using guide phrases to help them see that you are moving from one idea to another. Use phrases such as "now that we have seen how . . . , let us consider how . . ." and "my next argument. . . ." Terms such as *first, second, also, although,* and *however* will help your audience follow your line of thinking.

Use Repetition and Restatement   Repetition, restatement, and internal summaries will all help clarify your speech. Repetition means repeating something in exactly the same way. Restatement means rephrasing an idea or statement. Internal summaries are periodic summary statements or reviews of subsections of your speech. All will help listeners to follow what you are saying.

Notice how Donald M. Kendall (1986) uses an internal summary to achieve added clarity:

> The first three principles of management I've discussed—great people, with a shared vision, working in a decentralized but supportive organization—these tend to be somewhat internally focused. My fourth and final principle deals with the external focus of managing an organization. It's the importance of developing personal relationships.

Distinguish Between Commonly Confused Words   Many words, because they sound alike or are used in similar situations, are commonly confused. Learn these terms and avoid such confusions. Here are ten of the most frequently confused words:

- Use *accept* to mean *to receive* and *except* to mean *with the exclusion of* (*She accepted the award and thanked everyone except the producer*).
- Use *to affect* to mean *to have an effect* or *to influence* and *to effect* to mean *to produce a result* (*The teacher affected his students greatly and will now effect an entirely new curriculum*).
- Use *between* when referring to two items (*It is between this one and that one*) and *among* when referring to *more than two items* (*I want to choose from among these five items*).
- Use *can* to refer to *ability* and *may* to refer to *permission* (*I can scale the mountain but I may not reveal its hidden path*).
- Use *discover* to refer to the act of *finding something out* or *to learn something previously unknown* and use *invent* to refer to the act of *originating something new* (*We discover unknown lands but we invent time machines*).
- Use *explicit* to mean *specific* and *implicit* to mean the act of *expressing something without actually stating it* (*He was explicit in his denial of the crime but was implicit about his whereabouts*).
- Use *to imply* to mean *to state indirectly* and *to infer* to mean *to draw a conclusion* (*She implied that she would seek a divorce; we can only infer her reasons*).
- Use *precede* to mean *to go before* and use *proceed* to mean *to go ahead* (*In the graduation ceremony, the senior faculty members preceded the junior*

faculty members. You may proceed with your talk as soon as the audience set-tles down).

- Use *tasteful* to refer to one's *good taste* and use *tasty* to refer to something that tastes good (*The wedding was tasteful and the food most tasty*).
- Use *uninterested* to mean *a lack of interest* and use *disinterested* to mean *objective* or *unbiased* (*The student seemed uninterested in the lecture. The teacher was disinterested in who received what grades*).

Vividness

Select words to make your ideas vivid and come alive in the minds of your listeners.

Use Active Verbs   Favor verbs that communicate activity rather than passivity. The verb *to be* in all its forms—*is, are, was, were, will be*—is relatively inactive. Try using verbs of action instead. Rather than saying "The teacher was in the middle of the crowd," say "The teacher *stood* in the middle of the crowd." Instead of saying "The report was on the president's desk for three days," try "The report *rested* (or *slept*) on the president's desk for three days." Instead of saying "Management will be here tomorrow," consider "Management will descend on us tomorrow" or "Management jets in tomorrow."

Use Strong Verbs   The verb is the strongest part of your sentence. Choose verbs carefully, and choose them so they accomplish a lot. Instead of saying "He walked through the forest," consider such terms as *wandered, prowled, rambled,* or *roamed.* Consider whether one of these might not better suit your intended meaning. Look in a thesaurus for substitutes for any verb you suspect might be weak.

Use Figures of Speech   Figures of speech, stylistic devices that have been a part of rhetoric since ancient times, also help you achieve vividness. Table 8.1 contains a few such devices you might use in your speech, along with definitions and examples.

Use Imagery   Appeal to the senses, especially our visual, auditory, and tactile senses. Make us see, hear, and feel what you are talking about.

Visual Imagery   In describing people or objects, create images your listeners can see. When appropriate, describe such visual qualities as height, weight, color, size, shape, length, contour. Let your audience see the sweat pouring down the faces of the coal miners. Let them see the short, overweight executive in a pin-striped suit smoking a cigar. Here Stephanie Kaplan (Reynolds & Schnoor, 1991), a student from the University of Wisconsin, uses visual imagery to describe the AIDS Quilt:

> The Names Project is quite simply a quilt. Larger than 10 football fields, and composed of over 9 thousand unique 3 feet by 6 feet panels each bearing a name of an individual who has died of AIDS. The panels have been made in homes across the country by the friends, lovers, and families of AIDS victims.

Auditory Imagery   Appeal to our sense of sound by using terms that describe sounds. Let your listeners hear the car *screeching,* the wind *whistling,* the bells *chiming,* the angry professor *roaring.*

Table 8.1 Figures of Speech

Figure	Definition	Example
Alliteration	repetition of the same initial sound in two or more words	fifty famous flavors, the cool calculating leader.
Metaphor	the comparison of two unlike things	She's a lion when she wakes up; all nature is science; he's a real bulldozer
Metonymy	the substitution of a name for a title with which it is closely associated	City Hall issued the following news release where City Hall is used instead of the mayor or the city council
Rhetorical question	the use of a question to make a statement or to produce some desired effect rather than to secure an answer	Do you want to be popular? Do you want to get well?
Simile	the comparison of two unlike objects by using *like* or *as*	He takes charge like a bull; the manager is as gentle as a lamb
Synonymy	the repetition of synonyms for emphasis	the kind, warm, and generous teacher

Tactile Imagery   Use terms referring to temperature, texture, and touch to create tactile imagery. Let your listeners feel the cool water running over their bodies and the punch of the fighter. Let them feel the smooth skin of the newborn baby.

Appropriateness

Use language that is appropriate to you as the speaker, to your audience, to the occasion, and to the speech topic.

Speak on the Appropriate Level of Formality   The most effective public speaking style is less formal than the written essay. One way to achieve an informal style is to use contractions. Say *don't* instead of *do not*, *I'll* instead of *I will*, and *wouldn't* instead of *would not*. Contractions give a public speech the sound and rhythm of conversation, a quality that most listeners react to favorably.

Avoid written-style expressions such as "as explained below" or "the above-mentioned article" as well as expressions such as "the argument presented above." These make listeners feel you are reading to them rather than talking with them.

Use personal pronouns rather than impersonal expressions. Say "I found" instead of "it has been found," or "I will present three arguments" instead of "Three arguments will be presented."

Avoid Unfamiliar Terms   Avoid using terms the audience does not know. Avoid foreign and technical terms unless you are certain the audience is familiar with them. Similarly, avoid jargon (the technical vocabulary of a specialized field) unless you are sure the meanings are clear to your listeners. Some acronyms (NATO, UN, NOW, and CORE) are probably familiar to most audiences. Most, however, are not. When you wish to use any of these word types, explain fully their meaning to the audience.

Avoid Offensive Language   Avoid offending your audience with language that embarrasses them or makes them think you have little respect for them. Although your listeners may themselves use such expressions, they often resent their use by public speakers.

Avoid terms that your listeners might see as sexist, racist, or heterosexist. For example, avoid using the masculine pronoun to refer to the hypothetical person or terms such as *chairman, policeman,* or *salesman,* since these exclude women. Instead use *he and she* or plural forms; similarly, use non–gender-specific terms when referring to people in general, for example, *chairperson, police officer,* or *salesperson.*

Show this same equality to members of different races, nationalities, religions, and sexual orientations. Avoid referring to such groups with terms that carry negative connotations. Avoid picturing members of these groups in stereotypical and negative ways. But avoid slighting members of minority groups. Include references to minority groups and minority members in your examples and illustrations.

Personal Style

Audiences favor speakers who speak in a personal rather than an impersonal style, who speak *with* them rather than *at* them.

Use Personal Pronouns   As already noted, say *I* and *me* and *he* and *she* and *you.* Avoid such expressions as the impersonal *one* (as in "One is led to believe . . . ") or "this speaker," or "you, the listeners." These expressions distance the audience and create barriers rather than bridges.

Use Questions   Ask the audience questions to involve them. In a small audience, you might even briefly entertain responses. In larger audiences, you might ask the question, pause to allow the audience time to think, and then move on. When you direct questions to your listeners, they feel like a part of your speech.

Create Immediacy   Immediacy is a connectedness, a relatedness with one's listeners. Immediacy is the opposite of disconnected and separated. Create a sense of immediacy by using the "you approach." Say, "You'll enjoy reading . . . " instead of "Everyone will enjoy reading. . . . " Say, "I want you to see . . . " instead of "I want people to see. . . . "

Refer directly to commonalities between you and the audience; for example, "We are all children of immigrants." Say "We all want to see our team in the playoffs." Refer to shared experiences and goals; for example, "We all want, we all need a more responsive PTA."

Forcefulness/Power

Forceful or powerful language will help you achieve your purpose, whether it be informative or persuasive. Forceful language enables you to direct the audience's attention, thoughts, and feelings.

Eliminate Weakeners   Cut out phrases that weaken the strength of your sentences. Among the major weakeners are uncertainty expressions, disclaimers, and weak modifiers. *Uncertainty expressions* such as *I'm not sure of this but*, *perhaps it might*, or *maybe it works this way* communicate a lack of commitment and conviction and will make your audience wonder if you're worth listening to.

Disclaimers such as *I didn't read the entire article but* or *This is what I've heard* deny responsibility for your own statements and may lead listeners to question the validity of what you say.

Weak modifiers such as *It works pretty well, It's kind of like . . . ,* or *It may be the one we want* make you seem unsure and indefinite about what you are saying.

Vary Intensity as Appropriate   Much as you can vary your voice in intensity, you can also phrase your ideas with different degrees of stylistic intensity. You can, for example, refer to an action as "failing to support our position" or as "stabbing us in the back." You can say that a new proposal will "endanger our goals" or "destroy us completely." You can refer to a child's behavior as "playful," "creative," or "destructive." You can describe that child as "pretty" or as "beautiful." Vary your language to express different degrees of intensity—from mild through neutral to extremely intense.

Avoid Clichés   Clichés are phrases that have lost their novelty and part of their meaning through overuse. Clichés call attention to themselves because of their overuse. Here are some to avoid:

the whole ball of wax	by hook or by crook
in this day and age	sweet as sugar
tell it like it is	free as a bird
in the pink	no sooner said than done
tried and true	a horse of a different color
it goes without saying	few and far between
no news is good news	down in the mouth
the life of the party	keep your shirt on

PHRASING SENTENCES

Give the same careful consideration to your sentences that you give to your words. Here are some guidelines.

Use Short Sentences

Short sentences are more forceful and economical. They are easier to comprehend. They are easier to remember. Listeners do not have the time or the inclination to unravel long and complex sentences. Help them listen more efficiently by keeping your sentences brief.

Use Direct Sentences

Direct sentences are easier to understand. They are also more forceful. Instead of saying, "I want to tell you of the three main reasons why we should not adopt Program A," say, "We should not adopt Program A. There are three main reasons."

Use Active Sentences

Active sentences make your speech livelier and more vivid, and they clarify your point. Instead of saying "The lower court's decision was reversed by the Supreme Court," say "The Supreme Court reversed the lower court's decision." Instead of saying "The proposal was favored by management," say "Management favored the proposal."

Use Positive Sentences

Positive sentences are easier to comprehend and remember. Notice how sentences (a) and (c) are easier to understand than sentences (b) and (d).

(a) The committee rejected the proposal.
(b) The committee did not accept the proposal.
(c) This committee works outside the normal company hierarchy.
(d) This committee does not work within the normal company hierarchy.

CHAPTER **9**

DEVELOPING INTRODUCTIONS, CONCLUSIONS, AND TRANSITIONS

CHAPTER CONTENTS

Introductions
    Gain Attention
    Establish a Speaker-Audience-Topic Relationship
    Orient the Audience
    Some Common Faults of Introductions

Conclusions
    Summarize
    Motivate
    Provide Closure
    Some Common Faults of Conclusions

Before the Introduction and After the Conclusion

Transitions and Internal Summaries
    Transitions
    Internal Summaries

CHAPTER GOALS

After completing this chapter, you should be able to

1. construct introductions that gain attention, establish a speaker-audience-topic connection, and orient the audience

2. construct conclusions that summarize, motivate, and provide crisp closure

3. develop transitions and internal summaries to connect the major parts of your speech

Now that you have the body of your speech organized and have focused on styling your speech, devote your attention to your introduction, your conclusion, and the transitions that will hold the pieces of your speech together.

INTRODUCTIONS

Although you obviously will deliver the introduction to your speech first, you should construct it only after you have constructed the entire speech (body *and* conclusion). Begin collecting material for your introduction as you prepare the entire speech, but wait until all the other parts are completed before you put the pieces together. In this way you will be better able to judge which elements should be included.

Your introduction should serve three functions: gain attention, establish a speaker-audience-topic connection, and orient the audience as to what is to follow.

Gain Attention
You can secure attention in a number of ways; here are just a few examples.

Ask a Question   Richard Weaver (1991), in a speech on self-motivation delivered to fraternity members, uses a series of questions to gain attention and to focus it on his topic.

> Does it feel like you're being torn in all directions? Like you're getting stressed out? Like every teacher thinks his or her class is the *only* one you're taking? Like everything is coming down on you all at once, and you're not sure you can, or even want to, withstand the pressure? Do things feel like they are out of control? At least you know you're normal! Self-motivation is most likely to occur when you can successfully deal with the stresses in your life. Stress depletes both energy and motivation.

Refer to Audience Members   Harvey C. Jacobs (1985) gains attention by referring to members of the audience (and complimenting them) in his introduction:

> Winston Churchill once gave this advice to public speakers: One, never walk up a wall that's leaning against you; two, never try to kiss a person who's leaning away from you; and, three, never speak to a group that knows more about the subject than you do. You work much closer to the readers than I do. You know readers very well, I'm sure. Editors are often referred to as the ivory tower crowd, while circulation people are out in the trenches trying to peddle the product we editors and reporters create.

Refer to Recent Happenings   In a speech on the occasion of the minting of the $5 gold pieces commemorating the Statute of Liberty, Lee Iacocca, whose Chrysler Corporation had been recently hit by a strike, referred to this recent happening briefly and humorously:

> This is my second ceremony involving a strike this week and the first one didn't turn out so well.

Use Humor   A clever (and appropriate) joke or anecdote is always useful in holding attention. If you feel uncomfortable telling jokes in a public speaking situation, avoid this method. Similarly, avoid humor if you feel your joke or story will make any members of your audience uncomfortable. Further, make sure that your humor is integral to your speech topic. Use humor only if it relates directly to your specific speech topic. Here Peter Stark (1985) uses humor effectively in introducing his topic, networking:

> Have any of you ever wondered how you get to be a speaker at a Department of Social Services luncheon? So have I, so let me explain. It all started three months ago when Pat Letteri, your program coordinator, called and asked me how much I would charge to be a speaker on today's program. I told her my luncheon rates were $500 if she chooses the title and $250 if I choose the title. Either way, it would be the same speech. Well, Pat chose the $250 version and everything was fine until she called me two days ago. She stated there was a problem with the luncheon budget and I would have to renegotiate my price. Well, we negotiated and I am happy to report that I wrote a check to the Department of Social Services for $50 and here I am.

The speaker then connected this story with his speech topic, networking: the art of making and using interpersonal contacts.

Establish a Speaker-Audience-Topic Relationship

In addition to gaining attention, use your introduction to establish a connection among yourself as the speaker, the audience members, and your topic. Try to answer your listeners' inevitable question: why should we listen to you speak on this topic? You can establish an effective speaker-audience-topic relationship in a number of ways.

Establish Your Credibility   Here, for example, A. L. Jones (1972) establishes his credibility in his introduction in two ways. He establishes his good character by referring to his deep concern for the environment, and he establishes his competence by referring to his own studies in the field of ecology:

> For several years I have been deeply concerned about reports of the destruction of our environment as a result of technological recklessness, overpopulation, and a religious and philosophical outlook that gives little consideration to the preservation of nature. My studies in this area of concern have turned up evidence that I feel compelled to share with you. I welcome this opportunity to do it.

Refer to Others Present   Not only will this help you to gain attention, it will also help you to establish an effective speaker-audience-topic relationship. In this example Harvey Mackay (1991) refers not only to the audience but also to their present thoughts and feelings:

> I'm flattered to be here today, but not so flattered that I'm going to let it go to my head. Yes, I was delighted to be asked to be your commencement speaker. But I also know the truth: by the time you're my age ninety-nine out of a hundred will have completely forgotten who spoke at your graduation.
>
> And, I can accept that. Because I can't remember the name of my commencement speaker either. What I *do* remember from graduation day is the way I *felt*: excited, scared and challenged. I was wondering what the world was like out there, and how I would manage to make an impact.

Express Your Pleasure in Speaking   Yukio Matsuyama (1992) effectively establishes a speaker-audience-topic relationship by humorously expressing his pleasure in addressing the audience:

> I feel very happy to be invited here today. It is always a great pleasure for me to talk about Japan with those Americans who have a sincere interest in Japanese affairs and who don't find us inscrutable, but only intractable.

Compliment the Audience   Pay the audience an honest and sincere compliment, and they will not only give you their attention, they will also feel a part of your speech. In this example Eric Rubenstein (1992) compliments the audience directly by noting the group's accomplishments:

> Let me compliment your fine organization, Job Resources, on having counseled and job-trained more than 7,000 individuals, and having also obtained permanent employment for over 2,000 men and women since 1979.

Express Similarities with the Audience   By stressing your own similarity with members of the audience you create a bond with them and become an "insider" instead of an "outsider." Here Janice Payan (1990) uses this technique most effectively:

> Thank you. I felt as if you were introducing someone else because my mind was racing back 10 years, when I was sitting out there in the audience at the Adelante Mujer conference. Anonymous. *Comfortable*. Trying hard to relate to our "successful" speaker, but mostly feeling like Janice Payan, working mother, *glad for a chance to sit down*.
>
> I'll let you in on a little secret. I *still am* Janice Payan, working mother. The only difference is that I have a longer job title, and that I've made a few discoveries these past 10 years that I'm eager to share with you.
>
> The first is that keynote speakers at conferences like this are *not* some sort of alien creatures. Nor were they born under a lucky star. They are ordinary *Hispanic Women* who have stumbled onto an extraordinary discovery.

Orient the Audience

The introduction should orient the audience in some way to what is to follow in the body of the speech. Preview for the audience what you are going to say. The orientation may be covered in a variety of ways.

Give a General Idea of Your Subject   Here are just a few examples of the many ways in which you can give the audience a general idea of your speech subject:

> Tonight I'm going to discuss atomic waste.
> My concern today is with pollution.
> I want to talk with you about the problems our society has created for the aged.

Here Nannerl Keohane (1991) orients her audience by giving a general idea of the topic:

> My topic is leadership—a sorely needed skill in our country and our world these days; and particularly women leaders—an even scarcer phenomenon; and how we might prepare more women to be leaders in the future.

Give a Detailed Preview S. J. Buchsbaum (1991) provides a detailed orientation that previews what he will cover in his speech:

> Today, I want to review the problem of networked computer security, and establish some common perspectives on key aspects of this problem—along with some widely applicable security approaches. I will then discuss current forms of these security approaches in computer networks—ranging from very large computer networks, such as the AT&T telecommunications and information network, to the more limited computer networks that are pervading our corporate and national infrastructures. And I'll conclude with a look at emerging technological capabilities for improving computer network security.

Identify Your Goal Here, Harold Carr (1987) identifies in his introduction the thesis he hopes to establish:

> I'll argue today—and certainly will be happy to debate with you during the question session—that communications during a "crisis"—however you define that term—shouldn't be all that different from communications during routine times.

Here is another example:

> After hearing this speech, you will be able to use the new touch screen computers to access library information.

Introduce the Topic and Its Importance In this example, C. Ray Penn (1990) introduces his speech on the importance of words by stressing the topic's importance:

> "Sticks and stones may break my bones, but names will never hurt me"—this is the most quoted axiom about the effect of words upon human life. Of course it is much easier to say this to others than it is to have it said to us, even if the person intends it to make us feel better. The cruel fact of life is that if you ask a person to recall his or her most painful moment, it will most likely involve what someone said. . . .
>   "Sticks and stones may break my bones, but names will never hurt me"—it is my purpose today to replace these worn and dangerous words with another set of words—"A choice of words, is a choice of worlds."

Some Common Faults of Introductions

The introduction is perhaps the most important single part of the speech, so be especially careful to avoid the most common faults.

Don't Apologize A common fault is to apologize for *something.* Don't do it. You do not have to say, "I am not an expert on this topic" or "I didn't do as much reading on it as I should have." And *never* start a speech with "I'm not very good at giving public speeches." In your entire speech, but especially in your introduction, emphasize the positive; highlight your assets and your strengths. It is common in certain cultures—Japan is a good example—where speakers do begin with apologies. In these cultures, it is accepted and even expected. Here, then, is another good example of the need to know the culture and traditions of your audience.

Don't Rely on Gimmicks Avoid gimmicks that gain attention but are irrelevant to the nature of the speech or inconsistent with your treatment of the topic. For example, slamming a book on the desk or telling a joke that bears no relation to the rest of your speech may accomplish the very limited goal of gaining attention; but quickly the audience sees these techniques for what they are and will resent your attempt to fool them into paying attention.

Don't Preface Your Introduction   Do not preface your speech with such common but ineffective statements as these:

I'm really nervous, but here goes.
Before I begin my talk, I want to say. . . .
I hope I can remember everything I want to say.

CONCLUSIONS

Your conclusion is especially important because it is often the part of the speech that the audience remembers most clearly. It is your conclusion that in many cases determines what image of you is left in the minds of the audience. Devote special attention to this brief but crucial part of your speech. Let your conclusion serve three major functions.

Summarize

The summary function is particularly important in an informative speech and less so in persuasive speeches. You may summarize your speech in a variety of ways.

Restate Your Thesis   Here, in a speech on socially responsible investing, Clark Moeller (1984) restates his thesis in this brief summary method:

In summary, socially responsible investing is a viable strategy for making your investment behavior consistent with your principles and promoting social justice. And—you don't have to sacrifice a good return on your investment in the process.

Restate the Importance of the Topic   In a speech entitled "Corporate Fitness Programs Pay Off," Brenda W. Simonson (1986) restates her thesis:

It is estimated that within the next five years, 25 percent of all major corporations in the United States will have established some sort of fitness programming. Indeed, corporate fitness programming has come of age. There's no doubt about it—healthy employees work more and cost less and that's why managers will embrace fitness, not as a fringe benefit, but as an integral part of their regular personnel and health care policies. The message is clear—fitness means profits.

Restate Your Major Propositions   In a speech on compact disk technology, Barbara Seidl (Boaz & Brey, 1988), a student from the University of Wisconsin, restates her major propositions:

Now having acquired a basic understanding of CDI technology, its applications in a number of areas, and some of the concerns over its future acceptance, you should now be able to draw your own conclusions about participating in this interesting evolution, because you'll soon be encountering the grandchild of this odd little disc, this miracle music technology. Compact Disk Interactive (CDI)—its the next electronic revolution.

Motivate

In your conclusion you have the opportunity to give the audience one final push in the direction you wish them to take: to buy stock, vote a particular way, or change an attitude. Although this step is optional, you may find it useful in both informative and persuasive speeches.

Use Emotional Appeal   The emotional appeal conclusion, although widely used in religious speaking, is often seen as inappropriate in a classroom setting. On certain solemn occasions and with highly emotional issues, it may prove extremely effective. An example on a relatively light note is provided by New York Governor Mario Cuomo (1985) in his speech at Harvard Class Day:

> As you go, Harvard, so will go students all over America. So, in the words of a great American, go for it! All of you. Go for and with each other. Go against oppression and despair and indifference and lowered aspirations. Go with the certainty that your one life can make a difference and that together, you can shake and shape this country and this world. Go for it, Harvard. And go for it now!

Ask for a Specific Response   Another type of motivational appeal specifies what you want the audience to do after listening to your speech. Clarence Darrow (Peterson, 1965), in his summation speech in defense of Henry Sweet, a black charged with murder, directed his conclusion at motivating the jury to vote not guilty in a case that drew national and worldwide attention because of the racial issues involved. A vote of not guilty was in fact quickly returned by a jury of twelve white men.

> Gentlemen, what do you think of our duty in this case? I have watched day after day these black, tense faces that have crowded this court. These black faces that now are looking to you twelve whites, feeling that the hopes and fears of a race are in your keeping. This case is about to end, gentlemen. To them, it is life. Not one of their color sits on this jury. Their fate is in the hands of twelve whites. Their eyes are fixed on you, their hearts go out to you, and their hopes hang on your verdict. This is all. I ask you, on behalf of this defendant, on behalf of these helpless ones who turn to you, and more than that—on behalf of this great state, and this great city, which must face this problem and face it fairly—I ask you, in the name of progress and of the human race, to return a verdict of not guilty in this case!

Provide Directions for Future Action   Another type of motivational conclusion is to identify, often in general terms, the directions you wish the audience to take. Here is an example by David Archambault (1992), president of the American Indian College Fund, in a speech to the Rotary Club:

> Let us make this anniversary a time of healing and a time of renewal, a time to wipe away the tears. Let us—both Indian and non-Indian—put our minds together and see what life we can make for our children. Let us leave behind more hope than we found.

Provide Closure

The third function of your conclusion is to provide closure. Often your summary will accomplish this, but in some instances it will prove insufficient. End your speech with a conclusion that is crisp and definite. Make the audience know that you have definitely and clearly ended. You may achieve closure through a variety of methods.

Refer to Subsequent Events   Notice how effectively John R. Silber (1985) refers to subsequent events in his speech on higher education:

> Each of these three issues has relevance not only for Americans but for any country seriously concerned about higher education and its relation to democracy. They are not the only issues of importance I have raised today, but they form a basis for further discussion. I am looking forward to a fruitful exchange of ideas in the panels that will follow.

Pose a Challenge or Question   You may close your speech by leaving the audience with a provocative question to ponder or a challenge to consider. David T. Kearns (1987), Chief Executive Officer of Xerox, provides crisp closure with his briefly stated request:

> Ladies and gentlemen, let me leave you with this thought. Today's kindergartners will be the first high school graduates of the 21st century. Let's give them a head start on their future. Let's start now.

Another method is to pose a question and answer it by recapping your thesis and perhaps some of your major arguments or propositions. Here Jeff Sculley (Reynolds & Schnoor, 1991), a student from Bradley University, in an after-dinner speech on homophobia asks a question as a way of summing up his speech and then answers it:

> How can we avoid this horrible fate? By simply giving up on hatred and fear, and remembering that the greatest guarantor of our civil liberties is mutual toleration.

Refer Back to the Introduction   Effective closure is sometimes achieved by referring back to your introduction. Win Borden (1985), for example, used the following introduction in a commencement address:

> It was 20 years ago when I sat where you sit this morning. As I thought about my remarks for today, I tried to recall the essence of the commencement address at my graduation. I can't remember a word that was said, or even who the speaker was. It's humbling to think my remarks may leave such an indelible impression on your minds.

Borden then referred back to this introduction in his conclusion:

> People are always watching you, learning from you, and looking to you for inspiration. In other words, it *is* important how you play the game of life. If, sometime in the future, someone asks you to remember what was significant about your commencement speech, I hope that you will tell them you remember that. It is important how you play the game of life.

Some Common Faults of Conclusions

Because the conclusion is such an important part of your speech, be careful to avoid the common problems.

Don't Apologize or Dilute Your Position   Avoid apologizing for any inadequacies, real or imagined. Actually, apologies are not always ineffective. In the hands of the right person they may help to interject a needed note of modesty. In most cases, however, it is best not to apologize.

Also, avoid expressions that dilute your position such as

I know this is not that important, but. . . .
We really don't know enough about inflation to offer any real advice, but anyway. . . .
This information is probably dated, but it was all I could find.

Another way speakers dilute the impact of their speeches is to end with expressions like "That's all I have to say" or "That's it" or "Well, that's my speech." Expressions like these signal that you gave too little attention to your conclusion and may also communicate a discomfort with the public speaking situation.

Don't Introduce New Material You may, of course, give new expression to ideas covered in the body of the speech, but do not introduce new material in your conclusion. Instead, use your conclusion to reinforce what you have already said and to summarize your essential points.

Don't Drag Out Your Conclusion End your speech crisply. Avoid dragging out your conclusion or prefacing each statement of the conclusion with terms that lead the audience to think that this is the last statement. Expressions such as "in summary," "in conclusion," or "therefore" will often lead the audience to expect an ending. When you are ready to end, end.

BEFORE THE INTRODUCTION AND AFTER THE CONCLUSION

Although it is convenient to consider your speech as beginning with your introduction, it actually begins as soon as the audience focuses on you as speaker. Similarly, your speech does not end after you have spoken the last sentence. It ends only after the audience directs its focus away from you to another speaker or another project. Here are a few suggestions for dealing with the speech before the introduction and after the conclusion.

Display enthusiasm when you get up from your seat and walk to your speaking position. Display no signs of discomfort or displeasure. Your listeners will respond more favorably if they feel you are enjoying the experience. Stand in front of the audience with a sense of control.

Do not start your speech as soon as you get up from your seat or even as soon as you get to the front of the room. Survey your audience; engage their attention. Pause briefly, then begin your speech.

If there is a question period following your speech and you are in charge of it, pause after you have completed your conclusion, glance over your audience, and ask if there are any questions. If there is a chairperson who will recognize audience members, pause after your conclusion, and then nonverbally indicate to the chairperson that you are ready to entertain questions.

If there are no questions, pause after the last statement of your conclusion. Continue to maintain eye contact with the audience for a second or two and then walk (do not run) to your seat. Once you sit down, show no signs of relief, do not sigh, or in any other way indicate that you are relieved or pleased that the experience is over. Focus your attention on the chairperson or the next speaker or on whatever activity is taking place.

TRANSITIONS AND INTERNAL SUMMARIES

Remember that your audience will hear your speech just once. They must understand it as you speak it or lose it. Transitions and internal summaries help listeners understand your speech more effectively and efficiently.

Transitions

Transitions are words, phrases, or sentences that connect the various parts of your speech. They provide the audience with guideposts that help them follow the development of your thoughts and arguments. Use transitions in at least the following places:

- between the introduction and the body of the speech
- between the body and the conclusion
- between the main points in the body of your speech

Here are the major transitional functions and some stylistic devices that you might use to serve these functions.

To announce the start of a major proposition or piece of evidence:

- First, . . .
- A second argument. . . .
- A closely related problem. . . .
- If you want further evidence, look at. . . .
- Next, consider. . . .
- My next point. . . .
- An even more compelling argument. . . .

To signal that you are drawing a conclusion from previously given evidence and argument:

- Thus, . . .
- Therefore, . . .
- So, as you can see. . . .
- It follows, then, that. . . .

To alert the audience to your introducing a qualification or exception:

- But, . . .
- However, also consider. . . .

To remind listeners of what has just been said and that it is connected with another issue that will now be considered:

- In contrast to . . . , consider also. . . .
- Not only . . . , but also. . . .

- In addition to . . . , we need to look at. . . .
- Not only should we . . . , but we should also. . . .

To signal the part of your speech that you are approaching:

- By way of introduction. . . .
- In conclusion. . . .
- Now, let's discuss why we are here today. . . .
- So, what's the solution? What should we do?

Enhance your transitions by pausing between your transition and the next part of your speech. This will help the audience see that a new part of your speech is coming. You might also take a step forward or to the side after saying your transition to help reinforce the movement from one part of your speech to another.

Internal Summaries

Closely related to the transition and in some cases a special type of transition is the *internal summary*. An internal summary is a statement that summarizes what you have already discussed. It is a statement that usually summarizes some major subdivision of your speech. The "remember" summaries throughout *Human Communication* are examples of internal summaries. Their function is to summarize some major subdivision of a chapter. Incorporate a number of internal summaries into your speech— perhaps working them into the transitions connecting, say, the major arguments or issues.

An internal summary that is also a transition might look something like this:

The three arguments advanced here were (1) . . . , (2) . . . , (3). . . . Now, what can we do about them? I think we can do two things. First, . . .

Another example:

Inadequate recreational facilities, poor schooling, and lack of adequate role models seem to be the major problems facing our youngsters. Each of these, however, can be remedied and even eliminated. Here is what we can do.

Note that these brief passages remind the listeners of what they have just heard and preview for them what they will now hear. The clear connection in their minds will fill in any gaps that may have been created through inattention, noise, and the like.

CHAPTER 10

PERFECTING DELIVERY

CHAPTER CONTENTS

Speaking Extemporaneously
   Advantages and Disadvantages
   Extemporaneous Delivery and Conversation
   Guidelines for Speaking Extemporaneously
   Extemporaneous Speaking and Notes
Effective Voice
   Volume
   Rate
   Articulation and Pronunciation
   Pauses
Effective Bodily Action
   Eye Contact
   Facial Expression
   Posture
   Gestures
   Gross Movement
Rehearsal: Practicing and Improving Delivery

CHAPTER GOALS

After completing this chapter, you should be able to

1. use effectively the extemporaneous method for delivering a public speech

2. use vocal volume, rate, articulation and pronunciation, and pauses to reinforce your ideas effectively

3. use eye contact, facial expressions, posture, gestures, and gross bodily movement to reinforce your ideas

In this chapter we look at the process of speaking extemporaneously, the general principles that govern effectiveness in delivery, the ways you can use your voice and bodily action most effectively, and suggestions for rehearsing your speech.

SPEAKING EXTEMPORANEOUSLY

Some speeches are delivered impromptu, without any prior preparation. Some are memorized and some are written out word-for-word and read aloud. Although there are advantages and disadvantages to each of these methods, the method we recommend is to speak extemporaneously.

Extemporaneous delivery involves thorough preparation and a commitment to memory of the main ideas and their order. It may also involve a commitment to memory of the first and last few sentences of the speech. There is, however, no commitment to exact wording for the major parts of the speech.

Advantages and Disadvantages

The extemporaneous method is useful in most speaking situations. Good college lecturers use the extemporaneous method. They prepare thoroughly and know what they want to say and in what order they want to say it. But they have given no commitment to exact wording.

This method allows you to respond easily to feedback. Should a point need clarification, you can elaborate on it when it will be most effective. With this method it is easy to be natural because you are being yourself. It is the method that comes closest to conversation or, as some theorists have put it, enlarged conversation. With the extemporaneous method, you can move about and interact with the audience.

The major disadvantage is that you may stumble and grope for words. If you have rehearsed the speech a number of times, however, this is not likely to happen. Another disadvantage is that you cannot give the speech the attention to style that you can give it with other methods. You can get around this disadvantage too by memorizing those phrases you want to say exactly. There is nothing in the extemporaneous method that prevents your committing to memory selected phrases, sentences, or quotations.

Extemporaneous Delivery and Conversation

Although more formal than conversation, delivery in public speaking should have some of the most important features of conversation. These qualities are immediacy, expressiveness, and responsiveness to feedback.

Immediacy   Create a clear connection between yourself and each member of the audience. Make your listeners feel that you are talking directly and individually to each of them.

You can communicate immediacy both verbally and nonverbally. Here are a few ways to help you communicate immediacy:

- Join yourself to the audience with terms such as *we, us,* and *our.*
- Be especially responsive to audience feedback.
- Maintain appropriate eye contact with the audience members.

- Maintain a physical closeness that reinforces a psychological closeness.
- Stand with a direct and open body posture.

Expressiveness Communicate genuine involvement in the public speaking situation. Here are several ways you can show this quality of expressiveness.

- Express responsibility for your own thoughts and feelings.
- Vary your vocal rate, pitch, volume, and rhythm to communicate involvement and interest in the audience and in the topic.
- Allow your facial muscles and your entire body to reflect and echo this inner involvement.
- Use gestures to communicate involvement. Too few gestures may signal disinterest. Too many may communicate uneasiness, awkwardness, or anxiety.

Responsiveness to Feedback The most defining feature of conversation is responsiveness to feedback. As a speaker, read carefully the feedback signals being sent by the audience. And respond to these signals with verbal, vocal, and bodily adjustments. For example, respond to audience feedback signals communicating lack of comprehension or inability to hear with added explanation or increased volume.

Guidelines for Speaking Extemporaneously

In speaking extemporaneously, you may find it helpful to memorize three parts of your speech. Memorize your opening lines, perhaps the first few sentences; your closing lines, perhaps the last few sentences of the speech; and your major propositions and the order in which you will present them.

The memorized opening and closing lines will enable you to focus complete attention on the audience. Memorizing these parts will also put you more at ease. Once you know exactly what you will say in opening and in closing the speech, you will feel more in control. By memorizing the main ideas, you will feel in control of the speech and the speech-making situation. Also, you will not have to refer to notes when making your main points. After all, if you expect your audience to remember these points, surely you should remember them as well.

Extemporaneous Speaking and Notes

For many speeches it may be helpful to use notes. A few simple guidelines may help you avoid some of the common errors made in using notes.

Keep Notes to a Minimum The fewer notes you take with you, the better off you will be. Resist the temptation to bring with you the entire speech outline. You may rely on it too heavily and lose the direct contact with the audience. Instead, compose a delivery outline (p. 69), using only key words.

Use Notes with "Open Subtlety" Do not make them more obvious than necessary, but at the same time don't try to hide them from the audience. Do not gesture with your notes and thus make them more obvious than they need be. Use them openly and honestly but gracefully.

Do Not Allow Your Notes to Prevent Directness   When referring to your notes, pause to examine them. Then regain eye contact with the audience and continue your speech. Do not read from your notes, just take cues from them.

EFFECTIVE VOICE

Four dimensions of voice are especially significant to the public speaker: volume, rate, articulation and pronunciation, and pauses. Your manipulation of these elements will enable you to control your voice to maximum advantage.

Volume

Volume refers to the relative intensity of the voice. Loudness, on the other hand, refers to the perception of that relative intensity. In an adequately controlled voice, volume will vary according to a number of factors. For example, the distance between speaker and listener, the competing noise, and the emphasis the speaker wishes to give an idea will all influence volume.

One obvious problem is a voice that is too low. When speech is so low that listeners have to strain to hear, they will soon tire of spending so much energy. Be particularly careful that you don't fade away at the ends of your sentences. Make sure the audience is able to hear these at an appropriate volume. On the other hand, a voice that is too loud will prove disturbing because it intrudes on listeners' psychological space.

Rate

Rate refers to the speed with which you speak. Normally, rate is measured in the number of words or syllables spoken per minute. About 160 to 170 words per minute seems average for speaking as well as for reading aloud.

If you talk too fast you deprive your listeners of time they need to understand and digest what you are saying. If the rate is extreme, the listeners will simply not spend the time and energy needed to understand your speech. If your rate is too slow it will encourage your listeners to wander to matters unrelated to your speech. Speak at a pace that engages the listeners and allows them time for reflection but without boring them.

Articulation and Pronunciation

Articulation refers to the movements the speech organs make as they modify and interrupt the air stream you send from the lungs. Different movements of these speech organs (for example, the tongue, lips, teeth, palate, and vocal cords) produce different sounds. *Pronunciation* refers to the production of syllables or words according to some accepted standard, identified in any good dictionary.

Our concern here is with identifying and correcting some of the most common problems associated with faulty articulation and pronunciation.

Articulation Problems   The three major articulation problems are omission, substitution, and addition of sounds or syllables.

Errors of Omission   Omitting sounds or even syllables is a major articulation problem but one you can easily overcome with concentration and practice. Here are some examples:

Not This	This
gov-a-ment	gov-ern-ment
hi-stry	hi-story
wanna	want to
studyin	studying
a-lum-num	a-lum-i-num
hon-orble	hon-or-able
comp-ny	comp-a-ny
vul-ner-bil-ity	vul-ner-a-bil-ity

Errors of Substitution   Substituting an incorrect sound for the correct one is another easily corrected problem. Among the most popular are substituting [*d*] for [*t*] and [*d*] for [*th*]. Here are a few examples:

Not This	This
wader	waiter
dese	these
ax	ask
undoubtebly	undoubtedly
beder	better

Other common substitution errors are these:

Not This	This
ekcetera	*etcetera*
ramark	remark
lenth	length

Errors of Addition   When we make errors of addition, we add sounds where they do not belong. Some examples include:

Not This	This
acrost	across
athalete	athlete
Americer	America
idear	idea
filim	film
lore	law

If you make any of these errors, you can correct them by following these steps:

- Become conscious of our own articulation patterns (and the specific errors you are making).
- Listen carefully to the articulation of prominent speakers (for example, broad-casters).
- Practice the correct patterns until they become part of your normal speech behavior.

Pronunciation Problems   The major pronunciation problem is pronouncing sounds that should remain silent. For some words, the acceptable pronunciation is not to pronounce certain sounds, as in the following examples:

Not This	*This*
offten	offen
homage	omage
Illinois	Illinoi
evening	evning
burgalar	burglar
athalete	athlete
airaplane	airplane

The best way to deal with pronunciation problems is to look up in a good dictionary any words whose pronunciation you are not sure of. Learn to read the pronunciation key for your dictionary, and make it a practice to look up words you hear others use that seem to be pronounced incorrectly or that you wish to use yourself but are not sure how to pronounce.

Pauses

Pauses come in two basic types: filled and unfilled. Filled pauses are pauses in the stream of speech that we fill with vocalizations such as *-er, -um, -ah,* and the like. Even expressions such as *well* and *you know*, when used just to fill up silence, are called filled pauses. These pauses are ineffective and weaken the strength of your message. They will make you appear hesitant, unprepared, and unsure of yourself.

Unfilled pauses are silences interjected into the normally fluent stream of speech. Unfilled pauses can be especially effective if used correctly. Here are just a few examples of places where unfilled pauses—silences of a few seconds—should prove effective.

- Pause at transitional points to signal that you are moving from one part of the speech to another or from one idea to another.
- Pause at the end of an important assertion to allow the audience time to think about the significance of what you are saying.
- Pause after asking a rhetorical question to provide time so the audience can think of how they would answer the question.
- Pause before an important idea to help signal that what comes next is especially significant.

EFFECTIVE BODILY ACTION

Your body is a powerful instrument in your speech. You speak with your body as well as with your mouth. The total effect of the speech depends not only on what you say but also on the way you present it. Five aspects of bodily action are especially important: eye contact, facial expression, posture, gestures, and gross bodily movement.

Eye Contact

The most important single aspect of bodily communication is eye contact. Speakers who do not maintain enough eye contact appear distant, unconcerned, and less trustworthy than speakers who look directly at their audience. And, of course, without eye contact, you will not be able to secure that all-important audience feedback.

Maintain eye contact with the entire audience. Involve all listeners in the public speaking transaction. Communicate equally with the members on the left and on the right, in both the back and the front.

Use your eyes to communicate your commitment to and interest in what you're saying. Communicate your confidence and commitment by making direct eye contact; avoid staring blankly through your audience or glancing over their heads, at the floor, or out the window.

Facial Expression

Facial expressions are especially important in communicating emotions, your anger and fear, boredom and excitement, doubt and surprise. If you feel committed to and believe in your thesis, you will probably display your feelings appropriately and effectively.

Nervousness and anxiety, however, may at times prevent you from relaxing enough so that your emotions come through. With time and practice, however, you will relax, and the emotions you feel will reveal themselves appropriately and automatically.

Posture

When delivering your speech stand straight but not stiff. Try to communicate a command of the situation without communicating the discomfort that is actually quite common for beginning speakers.

Avoid the common mistakes of putting your hands in your pockets or leaning on the desk, the podium, or the chalkboard. With practice you will come to feel more at ease and will communicate this in the way you stand before the audience.

Gestures

Gestures help illustrate your verbal messages. You do this regularly in conversation. For example, when saying "Come here," you probably move your head, hands, arms, and perhaps your entire body to motion the listener in your direction. Your body as well as your verbal message say "Come here."

Avoid using your hands to preen, for example, fixing your hair or adjusting your clothing. Avoid fidgeting with your watch, ring, or jewelry. Avoid keeping your hands clasped in front or behind your back.

Effective bodily action is spontaneous and natural to you as the speaker, to your audience, and to your speech. If it seems planned or rehearsed, it will appear phony and insincere. As a general rule, don't do anything with your hands that doesn't feel right for *you*; the audience will recognize it as unnatural. If you feel relaxed and comfortable with yourself and your audience, you will generate natural bodily action without conscious and studied attention.

Gross Movement

Large bodily movements help to keep the audience and you more alert. Even when speaking behind a lectern, you can give the illusion of movement. You can step back or forward or flex your upper body so it appears you are moving more than you are.

Avoid moving too little or too much. Speakers who move too little often appear strapped to the podium, afraid of the audience, or too disinterested to involve themselves fully. With too much movement, the audience begins to concentrate on the movement itself, wondering where the speaker will wind up next.

Use gross movements to emphasize transitions and the introduction of a new and important assertion. Thus, when making a transition, you might take a step forward to signal that something new is coming. Similarly, this type of movement may signal the introduction of an important assumption, bit of evidence, or closely reasoned argument.

REHEARSAL: PRACTICING AND IMPROVING DELIVERY

Effective public speaking delivery does not come naturally. It takes practice. The goal of practice is for you to develop a delivery that will help you achieve the purposes of your speech. Rehearsal should enable you to see how the speech will flow as a whole and to make any changes and improvements you think necessary. Through practice you will learn the speech effectively and determine how best to present it to your audience. More specifically, your delivery goals should include at least the following:

- timing your speech so that you use the time allotted to you but do not run over your assigned time
- perfecting your volume and rate so that these work for you rather than against you
- checking your articulation and pronunciation to eliminate any possible errors
- incorporating pauses and other delivery notes at appropriate places in your delivery outline
- perfecting your bodily action: your eye contact, facial expressions, gestures, and gross movements

The following procedures should assist you in using your time most effectively.

Rehearse the speech as a whole. Do not rehearse the speech in parts. Rehearse it from getting out of your seat through the introduction, body, and conclusion to returning to your seat. Be sure to rehearse the speech with all the examples and illustrations (and audiovisual aids if any) included. This will enable you to connect the parts of the speech and to see how they interact with each other.

Time the speech during each rehearsal. Make the necessary adjustments on the basis of this timing.

Approximate the actual speech situation. Rehearse the speech under conditions as close as possible to those under which you will deliver it. If possible, rehearse the speech in the same room in which you will present it. If this is impossible, try to simulate the actual conditions as close as you can—in your living room or even bathroom. If possible, rehearse the speech in front of a few supportive listeners.

Incorporate changes and delivery notes. Make any changes in the speech that seem appropriate between rehearsals. Do not interrupt your rehearsal to make notes or changes. If you do, you may never experience the entire speech from beginning to end. While making these changes, note too any words whose pronunciation or articulation you wish to check. Insert pause notations, "slow down" warnings, and other delivery suggestions into your outline. If possible, record your speech (ideally, on videotape) so you can hear (and see) exactly what your listeners will hear (and see).

Rehearse often. Rehearse the speech as often as seems necessary. Two useful guides are these: (a) Rehearse the speech at least three or four times. Less than this is sure to be too little. (b) Rehearse the speech as long as your rehearsals result in improvements in the speech or in your delivery.

CHAPTER **11**

THE INFORMATIVE SPEECH

CHAPTER CONTENTS

The Speech of Description
  Strategies for Describing
  Developing the Speech of Description

The Speech of Definition
  Strategies for Defining
  Developing the Speech of Definition

The Speech of Demonstration
  Strategies for Demonstrating
  Developing the Speech of Demonstration

CHAPTER GOALS

After completing this chapter, you should be able to

1. construct a speech of description following the recommended strategies

2. construct a speech of definition following the recommended strategies

3. construct a speech of demonstration following the recommended strategies

Now that you have followed the nine steps for preparing your speech, we can look at the two major types of speeches and suggest some additional refinements. In this chapter we focus on the informative speech and look at the several types of informative speeches you may be expected to deliver.

THE SPEECH OF DESCRIPTION

When you describe, you are concerned with explaining an object or person or with explaining an event or process. Here are a few examples.

Describing an Object or Person

The structure of the brain
The contributions of Thomas Edison
The parts of a telephone
The layout of Philadelphia
The hierarchy of a corporation
The components of a computer system

Describing an Event or Process

Andrew: the hurricane of the nineties
The events leading to World War II
Organizing a bodybuilding contest
Putting a parade together
Castro's takeover of Cuba
How a newspaper is printed
The process of buying a house
Purchasing stock

Strategies for Describing

Here are some suggestions for describing objects and people, events and processes.

Select an Appropriate Thought Pattern   Consider using a spatial or a topical organization when describing objects and people. Consider using a temporal pattern when describing events and processes. For example, if you were to describe the layout of Philadelphia, you might start from the north and work down to the south (using a spatial pattern). If you were to describe the contributions of Thomas Edison, you might select the three or four major contributions and discuss each of these equally (using a topical pattern).

If you were describing the events leading up to World War II, you might use a temporal pattern and start with the earliest and work up to the most immediate. A temporal pattern would also be appropriate for describing how a hurricane develops or how a parade is put together.

Use a Variety of Descriptive Categories   Describe the object or event with lots of descriptive categories. Use physical categories and ask yourself such questions as these: What color is it? How big is it? What is it shaped like? How high is it? How much does it weigh? How long or short is it? What is its volume? How attractive or unattractive is it?

Also, consider its social, psychological, and economic categories. In describing a person, for example, consider such categories as friendliness-unfriendliness, warmth-coldness, rich-poor, aggressive-meek, and pleasant-unpleasant.

Consider Using Audiovisual Aids   Audiovisual aids will help you describe almost anything. Use them if you possibly can. In describing an object or person, show your listeners a picture. Show them pictures of the brain, the inside of a telephone, the skeleton of the body. In describing an event or process, create a diagram or flowchart to illustrate the various stages or steps. Show your listeners a flowchart representing the stages in buying stock, in publishing a newspaper, in putting a parade together.

Consider Who, What, Where, When, and Why   These categories are especially useful when you want to describe an event or process. For example, if you are going to describe how to purchase a house, you might want to consider the people involved (who), the steps you have to go through (what), the places you will have to go (where), the time or sequence in which each of the steps has to take place (when), and the advantages and disadvantages of buying the house (why).

Developing the Speech of Description

Here are two examples of how you might go about constructing a speech of description. In this first example, the speaker describes the four steps in reading a textbook. Each main point covers one of the major steps. The thought pattern is a temporal one. The speaker discusses the main points in the order in which they would normally occur. Here is how the body of such a speech might appear in outline form:

Specific purpose: *to describe the four steps in reading a textbook.*
Thesis: *You can increase your textbook reading effectiveness.*
(How can we increase our textbook reading effectiveness?)

   I. Preview the text.
  II. Read for understanding.
 III. Read for retention.
 IV. Review the text.

In delivering such a speech a speaker might begin by saying something like this:

There are four major steps we should follow in reading a textbook. We should preview the text, read for understanding, read for retention, and review what we have read. Let's look at each of these steps in more detail.

    The first step is to preview the text. Begin at the beginning and look at the table of contents. How is the book organized? What are the major parts of the text? . . .

In this second example, the speaker identifies four suggestions for increasing assertiveness (again, following a temporal sequence).

Specific purpose: *to describe how we can become more assertive.*
Thesis: *Assertiveness can be increased.* (How can assertiveness be increased?)

I.   Analyze assertive behaviors.
II. Record your own assertive behaviors.
III. Rehearse assertive behaviors.
IV. Act assertively.

THE SPEECH OF DEFINITION

What is leadership? What is a born-again Christian? What is the difference between sociology and psychology? What is a cultural anthropologist? What is safe sex? These are all topics for informative speeches of definition.

A definition is a statement of the meaning or significance of a concept or a term. Use definitions when you wish to explain difficult or unfamiliar concepts or when you wish to make a concept more vivid or forceful.

In defining a term or in giving an entire speech of definition you may focus on defining a term, a system or theory, or the similarities and/or differences among terms or systems. It may be a subject new to the audience or one familiar to them but presented in a new and different way. Here are some examples:

Defining a Term

What is psychology?
What is drug addiction?
What are the types of love?
What is censorship?
What is a Peace Corps volunteer?
What is political correctness?

Defining a System or Theory

What is behaviorism?
What are the parts of a generative grammar?
Confucianism: its major beliefs
The play theory of mass communication

Defining Similar and Dissimilar Terms or Systems

Communism and socialism: some similarities and differences
What do Catholics and Protestants have in common?
Oedipus and Electra: How do they differ?
Love and infatuation: their similarities
Freshwater and saltwater fishing

Strategies for Defining

Here are several suggestions for defining.

Use a Variety of Definitions   When explaining a concept, it is helpful to define it in a number of different ways. Here are some of the most important ways to define a term.

Define by Etymology   In defining the word *communication,* you might note that it comes from the Latin *communis,* meaning "common"; in "communicating" you seek to establish a commonness, a sameness, a similarity with another individual.

Define by Authority   You might define *lateral thinking* by authority and say that Edward deBono (1977), who developed lateral thinking in 1966, has noted that "lateral thinking involves moving sideways to look at things in a different way. Instead of fixing on one particular approach and then working forward from that, the lateral thinker tries to find other approaches."

Define by Operations   An operational definition is perhaps the most important method of definition, in which you define an object by showing the operations one would go through in constructing it. Thus, to define a chocolate cake operationally, you would provide the recipe. The operational definition of stuttering would include an account of how the act of stuttering is performed and by what procedures stuttering might be observed.

Define by Negation   You might also define a term by noting what the term is not, that is, defining by negation. "A teacher," you might say, "is not someone who tells you what you should know but rather one who. . . . " Here Michael Marien (1992) defines *futurists* first negatively and then positively:

> Futurists do not use crystal balls. Indeed, they are generally loathe to make firm predictions of what will happen. Rather, they make forecasts of what is probable, sketch scenarios of what is possible, and/or point to desirable futures—what is preferable and what strategies we should pursue to get there.

Define by Direct Symbolization   In using this technique, you show the actual object you are defining or some picture or model of it.

Use Definitions to Add Clarity   If the purpose of the definition is to clarify, then it must do just that. Avoid defining terms that do not need extended definitions or defining terms with words that are so complex they also need defining. In the following excerpt Frederick Buchstein (1988) uses a humorous anecdote to add the necessary clarity and to distinguish the subject of his talk, public relations, from other related terms:

> This anecdote from *Reader's Digest* illustrates the difference between advertising and other corporate communications: "If you work for a circus and put 'The Circus is Coming to Town on Monday' posters all over town, that's advertising. If you put the posters on an elephant and parade him through the town, that's sales promotion. If you lead the elephant through the mayor's flower garden, that's publicity. If you can get the mayor to smile about it, that's public relations."

Use Credible Sources   When you use an authority to define a term, make sure the person is in fact an authority. Tell the audience who the authority is and the basis for the individual's expertise. In the following excerpt, note how Russell Peterson (1985) uses the expertise of Robert McNamara in his definition:

> When Robert McNamara was president of the World Bank, he coined the term "absolute poverty" to characterize a condition of life so degraded by malnutrition, illiteracy, violence, disease and squalor, to be beneath any reasonable definition of human decency. In 1980, the World Bank estimated that 780 million persons in the developing countries lived in absolute poverty. That's about three times as many people as live in the entire United States.

Proceed from the Known to the Unknown   Start with what your audience knows and work up to what is new or unfamiliar. Let's say you wish to explain the concept of *phonemics* (with which your audience is totally unfamiliar). The specific idea you wish to get across is that each phoneme stands for a unique sound. You might proceed from the known to the unknown and begin your definition with something like this:

> We all know that in the written language each letter of the alphabet stands for a unit of the written language. Each letter is different from every other letter. A *t* is different from a *g* and a *g* is different from a *b* and so on. Each letter is called a "grapheme." In English we know we have 26 such letters.
>
> We can look at the spoken language in much the same way. Each sound is different from every other sound. A *t* sound is different from a *d* sound and a *d* sound is different from a *k* sound, and so on. Each individual sound is called a "phoneme." In English we have approximately 42 such sounds or phonemes.
>
> Now, let me explain in a little more detail what I mean by a "phoneme."

In this way, you will build on what the audience already knows, a procedure that is useful in all learning.

Note how Richard Weaver (1987) relates his definition of creativity to what the audience already knows:

> All right, let me give you a little quiz. When was the last time you came up with a creative idea? This morning? Yesterday? Last week? Last month? Last year? What was it? What is it that motivates you to be creative?
>
> Some of the answers might be: "I found a new way to debug a computer program." "I decorated my room with a new poster." "I got a unique idea for a paper I had to write, or a speech that I had to give." "I found a new way to make lasagna taste even better." "I found a quicker way to get from my dorm room to McDonald's or Wendy's." Being creative is fun, and being creative results in change.

Developing the Speech of Definition

Here are two examples of how you might go about constructing a speech of definition. In this first example, the speaker selects three major types of lying for discussion and arranges these in a simple topical pattern.

Specific purpose: *to define lying by explaining the major types of lying misdirection.*

Thesis: *There are three major kinds of lying.* (What are the three major kinds of lying?)

   I.   Concealment is the process of hiding the truth.
  II.   Falsification is the process of presenting false information as if it were true.
 III.   Misdirection is the process of acknowledging a feeling but misidentifying its cause.

In delivering such a speech, a speaker might begin the speech by saying:

> A lie is a lie is a lie. True? Well, not exactly. Actually, there are a number of different ways we can lie. We can lie by concealing the truth. We can lie by falsification, by presenting false information as if it were true. And, we can lie by misdirection, by acknowledging a feeling but misidentifying its cause. Let's look at the first type of lie—the lie of concealment.

Most lies are lies of concealment. Most of the time when we lie, we don't actually make any false statements. Rather we simply don't reveal the truth. Let me give you some examples I overheard recently.

In this next example, the speaker explains the parts of a résumé and follows a spatial order, going from the top to the bottom of the page.

> *Specific purpose:* *to define the essential parts of a résumé.*
> *Thesis:* *There are four major parts to a résumé.* (What are the four major parts of a résumé?)

I. Identify your career goals.
II. Identify your educational background.
III. Identify your work experience.
IV. Identify your special competencies.

THE SPEECH OF DEMONSTRATION

In using demonstration (or in a speech devoted entirely to demonstration), you would explain how to do something or how something operates. Here are some examples:

Demonstrating How to Do Something

Giving mouth-to-mouth resuscitation
Balancing a checkbook
Piloting a plane
Driving defensively
Mixing colors
Developing your body

Demonstrating How Something Operates

How the body maintains homeostasis
The workings of a thermostat
How a heart bypass operation is performed

Strategies for Demonstrating

In demonstrating how to do something or how something operates, consider the following guidelines.

Use Temporal Organization In most cases, a temporal pattern will work best in speeches of demonstration. Demonstrate each step in the sequence in which it is to be performed. In this way, you will avoid one of the major difficulties in demonstrating a process—backtracking. Do not skip steps even if you think they are familiar to the audience. They may not be.

Connect each step to the next with appropriate transitions. For example, in explaining the Heimlich maneuver you might say:

Now that you have your arms around the chocking victim's chest, your next step is to. . . .

Assist your listeners by labeling the steps clearly by saying, for example, "the first step," "the second step," and so on.

Begin with an Overview   It is often helpful when demonstrating to give a broad general picture and then present each step in turn. For example, let's say you were talking about how to prepare a wall for painting. You might begin with a general overview and say this:

> In preparing the wall for painting, you want to make sure that the wall is smoothly sanded, free of dust, and dry. Sanding a wall is not like sanding a block of wood. So let's look at the proper way to sand a wall.

In this way, your listeners will have a general idea of how you will go about demonstrating the process.

Consider Using Visual Aids   Visual aids are often helpful in showing the steps of a process in sequence. A good example of this are the signs in restaurants demonstrating the Heimlich maneuver. These signs demonstrate each of the steps with pictures as well as words. The combination makes it easy for us to understand this important process.

Developing the Speech of Demonstration

Here are two examples of the speech of demonstration. In the first example, the speaker demonstrates how to listen actively.

Specific purpose: *to demonstrate three techniques of active listening.*
        Thesis: *We can learn active listening.* (How can we learn active listening?)

I.   Paraphrase the speaker's meaning.
II. Express understanding of the speaker's feelings.
III. Ask questions.

In delivering the speech, the speaker might begin by saying something like this:

> Active listening is a special kind of listening. It is listening with total involvement, with a concern for the speaker. Active listening consists of three steps: paraphrasing the speaker's meaning, expressing understanding of the speaker's feelings, and asking questions.
>   Your first step in active listening is to paraphrase the speaker's meaning. What is a paraphrase? A paraphrase is a restatement in your own words of the speaker's meaning. That is, you express in your own words what you think the speaker meant. For example, . . .

In this next example, the speaker explains the proper way to argue by identifying the ways we should *not* argue. As you can see, these unproductive fight strategies are all about equal in value and are arranged in a topical order.

Specific purpose: *to demonstrate how to fight fairly by identifying and demonstrating four unfair conflict strategies.*
        Thesis: *Conflict can be made more productive.* (How can conflict be made more productive?)

I.   Blame the other person.
II. Unload all your previous grievances.
III. Make light of the other person's displeasure.
IV. Hit the other person with issues he or she cannot handle effectively.

CHAPTER 12

THE PERSUASIVE SPEECH

CHAPTER CONTENTS

The Speech to Strengthen or Change Attitudes or Beliefs
  Strategies for Strengthening or Changing Attitudes and Beliefs
  Developing the Speech to Strengthen or Change Attitudes and
    Beliefs
The Speech to Move to Action
  Strategies for Moving Listeners to Action
  Developing the Speech to Actuate

CHAPTER GOALS

After completing this chapter, you should be able to

1. construct a persuasive speech to strengthen or change attitudes and beliefs following the recommended strategies

2. construct a persuasive speech to move listeners to action following the recommended strategies

Most of the speeches you hear are persuasive speeches. The speeches of politicians, advertisers, and religious leaders are perhaps the clearest examples. In most of your own speeches, you too will aim at persuasion. You will try to change your listeners' attitudes and beliefs or perhaps change their behaviors. In school you might try to persuade others to (or not to) expand the core curriculum, use a plus-minus or a pass-fail grading system, disband the basketball team, allocate increased student funds for the school newspaper, establish competitive majors, or eliminate fraternity hazing. On your job you may be called upon to speak for or against having a union, a wage-increase proposal, a health benefit package, or Tim Doolan for shop steward.

Persuasive speaking is and will continue to be an important part of your academic and professional life. Your persuasive abilities will enable you to achieve your goals more effectively and will help to distinguish you as a leader. In this chapter we examine the two major types of persuasive speeches.

THE SPEECH TO STRENGTHEN OR CHANGE ATTITUDES OR BELIEFS

Many speeches seek to strengthen existing attitudes or beliefs, such as those given by religious or political leaders. People who listen to religious speeches usually are already believers, so these speeches strive to strengthen the attitudes and beliefs the people already hold. Here the audience is already favorable to the speaker's purpose and is willing to listen.

Speeches designed to change attitudes or beliefs are much more difficult to construct. Most people resist change. When you try to get people to change their beliefs or attitudes you are fighting an uphill (but not impossible) battle.

Such speeches come in many forms. Depending on the initial position of the audience, you can view the following examples as topics for speeches to strengthen or change attitudes or beliefs.

> Marijuana should be legalized.
> General education requirements should be abolished.
> College athletic programs should be expanded.
> History is a useless study.
> Television shows are mindless.
> Records should be rated for excessive sex and violence.
> Puerto Rico should become the fifty-first state.

Strategies for Strengthening or Changing Attitudes and Beliefs

When you try to strengthen or change your listeners' attitudes and beliefs, consider the following principles.

Estimate Listeners' Attitudes and Beliefs   Carefully estimate—as best you can—the current state of your listeners' attitudes and beliefs. If your goal is to strengthen these attitudes, then you can state your thesis and your objectives as early in your speech as you wish. Since your listeners are in basic agreement with you, your statement of your thesis will enable you to create a bond of agreement between you.

You might say, for example:

> Like you, I am deeply committed to the fight against abortion. Tonight, I'd like to explain some new evidence that has recently come to light that we must know if we are to be effective in our fight against legalized abortion.

If, however, you are in basic disagreement and you wish to change their attitudes, then reserve your statement of your thesis until you have provided them with your evidence and argument. Get them on your side first by stressing as many similarities between you and your audience as you can. Only afterward should you try to change their beliefs. Continuing with the abortion example (but this time with an audience that is opposed to your antiabortion stance), you might say:

> We are all concerned with protecting the rights of the individual. No one wants to infringe on the rights of anyone. And it is from this point of view—from the point of view of the inalienable rights of the individual—that I want to examine the abortion issue.

In this way, you stress your similarity with the audience before you state your antiabortion position to this proabortion audience.

Seek Small Changes   When addressing an audience that is opposed to your position and your goal is to change their attitudes and beliefs, seek change in small increments. Let's say that your ultimate goal is to get an antiabortion group to favor abortion on demand. Obviously, this goal is too great to achieve in one speech. Therefore, strive for small changes. In this example the speaker attempts to get an antiabortion audience to agree that some abortions should be legalized. The speaker begins as follows:

> One of the great lessons I learned in college was that most extreme positions are wrong. Most of the important truths lie someone between the extreme opposites. And today I want to talk with you about one of these truths. I want to talk with you about rape and the problems faced by the mother carrying a child conceived in this most violent of all the violent crimes we can imagine.

Notice that the speaker does not state a totally proabortion position but instead focuses on one area of abortion and tries to get the audience to agree that in some cases abortion should be legalized.

Other strategies might involve persuading the audience to believe that those who favor abortion should be allowed equal advertising time. Or, you might seek to persuade your audience to be willing to watch a specific proabortion movie with an open mind. If you try to accomplish too much change, the audience will resist your arguments and resent your attempts.

Demonstrate Your Credibility   Show the audience that you are knowledgeable about the topic, have their own best interests at heart, and that you are willing and ready to speak out in favor of these important concerns.

Give Listeners Good Reasons   Give your audience good reasons for believing what you want them to believe. Give them hard evidence and arguments. Show them how such attitudes and beliefs relate directly to their goals, their motives.

Developing the Speech to Strengthen or Change Attitudes and Beliefs

Here are some examples to clarify the nature of this type of persuasive speech. In these examples we present the specific purpose, the thesis, and the question we ask of the thesis to help us identify the major propositions of the speech. In the first example, the speaker uses a problem-solution organizational pattern, first presenting the problems created by cigarette smoking, and then the solution.

Specific purpose: *to persuade my audience that cigarette advertising should be banned from all media.*

Thesis: *Cigarette advertising should be abolished.* (Why should it be abolished?)

I.   Cigarette smoking is a national problem.
  A.   Cigarette smoking causes lung cancer.
  B.   Cigarette smoking pollutes the air.
  C.   Cigarette smoking raises the cost of health care.

II.   Cigarette smoking will be lessened if advertisements are prohibited.
  A.   Fewer people would start to smoke.
  B.   Smokers would smoke less.

In delivering such a speech a speaker might begin like this:

I think we all realize that cigarette smoking is a national problem that affects each and every one of us. No one escapes the problems caused by cigarette smoking—not the smoker and not the nonsmoker. Cigarette smoking causes lung cancer. Cigarette smoking pollutes the air. And cigarette smoking raises the cost of health care for everyone.

Let's look first at the most publicized of all smoking problems: lung cancer. There can be no doubt—the scientific evidence is overwhelming—that cigarette smoking is a direct cause of lung cancer. Research conducted by the American Cancer Institute and by research institutes throughout the world all come to the same conclusion: cigarette smoking causes lung cancer. Consider some of the specific evidence. A recent study—reported in the November 1994 issue of the. . . .

In this example, dealing with birth control, a topical organizational pattern is used.

Specific purpose: *to persuade my audience that advertisements for birth control devices should be allowed in all media.*

Thesis: *Media advertising of birth control devices is desirable.* (Why is media advertising desirable?

I.   Birth control information is needed.
  A.   Birth control information is needed to prevent disease.
  B.   Birth control information is needed to prevent unwanted pregnancies.

II.   Birth control information is not available to the very people who need it most.
III.   Birth control information can best be disseminated through the media.

The speaker in the next example attempts to persuade the audience that the drinking age should be set at 18 by refuting the arguments against the 18-year-old standard. The assumption made by the speaker is that if these reasons are shown to be invalid, then the audience will be convinced that the 18-year-old standard should be accepted.

> *Specific purpose:*   *to persuade my audience that the drinking age should be lowered to 18.*
>   *Thesis:*   *The drinking age should be lowered to 18. (*Why should the drinking age be lowered to 18?*)*

I. The present system encourages disrespect for the law.
II. The present system encourages private drinking.
III. The present system does not prevent 18-, 19-, and 20-year-olds from drinking.

THE SPEECH TO MOVE TO ACTION

Speeches designed to move the audience to action or to engage in some specific behavior are referred to as *speeches to actuate*. The persuasive speech addressed to motivating a specific behavior may focus on just about any behavior imaginable. Here are some examples:

Vote in the next election.
Vote for Smith.
Do not vote for Smith.
Give money to the American Cancer Society.
Major in economics.
Take a course in computer science.
Buy a Pontiac.

Strategies for Moving Listeners to Action

When designing a speech to get listeners to do something, keep the following principles in mind.

Be Realistic   Be realistic in what you want the audience to do. Remember you have only 10 or 15 minutes and in that time you cannot move the proverbial mountain. Ask for small, easily performed behaviors—to sign a petition, to vote in the next election, to donate a small amount of money.

Demonstrate Your Own Compliance   As a general rule, never ask the audience to do what you have not done yourself, a rule our encyclopedia sales representative obviously didn't learn. If you haven't done what you suggest your listeners do, the audience will rightly ask, "Why haven't you done it?" In addition, show them that you are pleased to have done so. Tell them of the satisfaction you derived from donating blood or from reading to blind students.

For example, when I taught psycholinguistics I included a section on behavior modification. But before I taught the section on controlling one's own behavior I applied the principles of behavior control to my own smoking and stopped smoking myself. From an average of 58 cigarettes a day, I went to none (and remain a nonsmoker) through the application of these principles. Whenever I talk on behavior control, I use this personal example because it demonstrates more clearly than any research study I could cite that the principles work and that I am personally committed to such a program of behavior control.

Stress Specific Advantages   Stress the specific advantages of these behaviors to your specific audience. Don't ask your audience to engage in behaviors solely because of some abstract reason. Give them concrete, specific reasons why they will benefit from the actions you want them to engage in. Instead of telling your listeners that they should devote time to reading to blind students because it is the right thing to do, show them how much they will enjoy the experience and how much they will personally benefit from the experience.

Developing the Speech to Actuate

Here are a few examples of the speech to actuate. In this first example the speaker tries to persuade the audience to buy a personal computer.

Specific purpose: *to persuade my audience to buy a personal computer.*
        Thesis: *Personal computers are useful. (*Why are personal computers useful? *or* In what ways are personal computers useful?*)*

   I.   Personal computers are useful for word processing.
      A.   You can type faster with a word processor.
      B.   You can revise documents easily with a word processor.

  II.   Personal computers are useful for bookkeeping.
III.   Personal computers are useful for research.

In delivering such a speech a speaker might say:

Have you ever added up all the hours you have spent typing your college papers? Have you ever tried to keep your finances in order only to lose the little pieces of paper you wrote your figures on? And then you had to start all over again. Have you ever gone to our college library and not found what you were looking for? Or, maybe I should say, have you ever gone to our library and found exactly what you were looking for?

     Typing, bookkeeping, and research are a computer's three greatest strengths and I'd like to tell you in more detail about how a computer can simplify your life. I'm sure that by the end of this brief talk you will want to run, not walk, to your nearest computer dealer and buy your own personal computer.

     I think typing is probably the most boring of all college chores. . . .

Here is a speech on devoting time to help the handicapped. Here the speaker asks for a change in the way most people spend their leisure time. It utilizes a topical thought pattern; each of the subtopics is treated about equally.

Specific purpose: *to persuade my audience to devote some of their leisure time to helping the handicapped.*
        Thesis: *Leisure time can be well used in helping the handicapped. (*How can leisure time be spent helping the handicapped? *or* What can we do to help the handicapped?*)*

   I.   Read for the blind.
      A.   Read to a blind student.
      B.   Make a recording of a textbook for blind students.

   II.   Run errands for students confined to wheelchairs.

   III.   Type for students who can't use their hands.

In this next example, the speaker asks for a specific action, namely, that the audience members take a specific course. The speech follows a topical thought pattern.

> *Specific purpose:*   *to persuade my audience to elect a course in Small Group Communication.*
>
>   *Thesis:*   *Small Group Communication is a great elective course.*
>   (Why is Small Group Communication a great elective course?)

   I.   Small Group Communication is enjoyable.
- A.   Small Group received an extremely high rating in the Student Evaluation Guide.
- B.   My entire class enjoyed it.

   II.   Small Group Communication is practical.
- A.   You'll learn problem-solving skills.
- B.   You'll learn interviewing skills.
- C.   You'll learn consciousness-raising skills.

POSTSCRIPT

In these 12 brief chapters, we've covered the practical principles of public speaking. You may wish to reflect on some of the most important skills that will serve you throughout your college and professional career:

- to select and limit topics as appropriate to your purpose and your audience
- to analyze a wide variety of audiences and effectively adapt your speeches to their unique characteristics and attitudes
- to research a wide variety of topics effectively and efficiently
- to organize materials into a meaningful and coherent speech
- to support your ideas so that they are understandable and persuasive
- to develop your own credibility—competence, character, and charisma
- to evaluate public speeches critically—their arguments, appeals, and impact
- to give criticism to others that is constructive and supportive
- to word messages so that they are clear, persuasive, and easily remembered by the audience
- to deliver public speeches to a wide variety of audiences with effective voice and bodily action

Put differently, you should be able to construct and deliver effective informative and persuasive speeches and function effectively as a critic of public communication.

BIBLIOGRAPHY

Akinnaso, F. Niyi (1982). On the Differences between Spoken and Written Language. *Language and Speech* 25, Part 2:97–125.

Alisky, Marvin (1985, January 15). *Vital Speeches of the Day* 51.

Allen, Mike and Raymond W. Preiss (1990, April). Using Meta-analysis to Evaluate Curriculum: An Examination of Selected College Textbooks. *Communication Education* 38:103–116.

The American Public and the Income Tax System (1978). Kansas City, MO: H. & R. Block.

Archambault, David (1992, June 1). *Vital Speeches of the Day* 491–493.

Banach, William J. (1991, March 15). Are You Too Busy to Think? *Vital Speeches of the Day* 351–352.

Beebe, S. A. and J. T. Masterson (1990). *Communicating in Small Groups: Principles and Practices,* 3rd ed. New York: Harper-Collins.

Bem, Sandra L. (1974). The Meaure of Psychological Androgyny. *Journal of Consulting and Clinical Psychology* 42:155–162.

Bem, Sandra L. (1981). Gender Schema Theory. *Psychological Review* 88:354–371.

Boaz, John K. and James R. Brey, eds. (1987). *1987 Championship Debates and Speeches.* Normal, IL: American Forensic Association.

Boaz, John K. and James R. Brey, eds. (1988). *1988 Championship Debates and Speeches.* Normal, IL: American Forensic Association.

Borden, Win (1985, April 15). *Vital Speeches of the Day* 51.

Boster, Frank and Peter Mongeau (1984). Fear Arousing Persuasive Messages. In Robert Bostrom, ed., *Communication Yearbook 8.* Newbury Park, CA: Sage, 330–377.

Brickfield, Cyril F. (1985, August 1). *Vital Speeches of the Day* 51.

Buchstein, Frederick (1988, June 15). *Vital Speeches of the Day* 534–536.

Buchsbaum, S. J. (1991, December 15). *Vital Speeches of the Day* 150–155.

Bush, George (1988, October 15). *Vital Speeches of the Day* 55.

Butcher, Willard C. (1987, September 1). *Vital Speeches of the Day* 680.

Buscaglia, Leo (1988, June 28). *Woman's Day.*

Canary, Daniel J. and Kimberley S. Hause (1993). Is There Any Reason to Research Sex Differences in Communication? *Communication Quarterly* 41:129–144.

Carr, Harold (1987, February 1). *Vital Speeches of the Day* 53.

Chisholm, Shirley (1978, August 15). *Vital Speeches of the Day.*

Cuomo, Mario (1985, July 15). *Vital Speeches of the Day* 51.

deBono, Edward (1977). *Wordpower.* New York: Harper Colophon.

Delattre, Edwin (1988, May 15). *Vital Speeches of the Day* 467.

DeVito, Joseph A. (1969). Some Psycholinguistic Aspects of Active and Passive Sentences. *Quarterly Journal of Speech* 55:401–406.

Gonzalez, A. and P. G. Zimbardo (1985, April). Time in Perspective. *Psychology Today* 19:20–26.

Gronbeck, Bruce E., Raymie E. McKerrow, Douglas Ehninger, and Alan H. Monroe (1990). *Principles and Types of Speech Communication,* 11th ed. New York: HarperCollins.

Guerra, Stella (1986, September 15). *Vital Speeches of the Day* 727.

Howard, Carole (1984, December 15). *Vital Speeches of the Day* 51:148–150.

Jackson, William (1985, September 15). *Vital Speeches of the Day.*

Jacobs, Harvey C. (1985, May 1). *Vital Speeches of the Day* 51.

Johnson, Geneva B. (1991, April 15). *Vital Speeches of the Day* 393–398.

Jones, A. L. (1972, April 1). *Vital Speeches of the Day* 38.

Kearns, David T. (1987, December 15). *Vital Speeches of the Day* 54.

Keohane, Nannerl O. (1991, July 15). *Vital Speeches of the Day* 605–608.

Lamkin, Martha (1986, December 15). *Vital Speeches of the Day* 152.

Loden, Marilyn (1986, May 15). *Vital Speeches of the Day* 472– 475.

Lunsford, Charlotte (1988, September 15). *Vital Speeches of the Day* 731.

Mackay, Harvey B. (1991, August 15). *Vital Speeches of the Day* 656–659.

Marien, Michael (1984, March 15). *Vital Speeches of the Day* 340–344.

Matsuyama, Yukio (1992, May 15). *Vital Speeches of the Day* 461– 466.

McNamara, Robert (1985, July 1). *Vital Speeches of the Day* 549.

Moeller, Clark (1984, August 15). *Vital Speeches of the Day* 54.

Nelson, Alan (1986). *Vital Speeches of the Day* 52.

Orski, C. Kenneth (1986, February 1). *Vital Speeches of the Day* 274.

Osborn, Alex (1957). *Applied Imagination,* rev. ed. New York: Scribner's.

Payan, Janice (1990, September 1). *Vital Speeches of the Day* 697–701.

Penn, C. Ray (1990, December 1). *Vital Speeches of the Day* 116–117.

Peterson, Huston, ed. (1965). *A Treasury of the World's Great Speeches.* New York: Simon & Schuster.

Peterson, Russell W. (1985, July 1). *Vital Speeches of the Day* 549.

Quayle, Dan (1988, October 15). *Vital Speeches of the Day* 51.

Reynolds, Christina L. and Larry G. Schnoor, eds. (1991). *1989 Championship Debates and Speeches.* Normal, IL: American Forensic Association.

Rockefeller, David (1985, March 15). *Vital Speeches of the Day* 328–331.

Rubenstein, Eric (1992, April 15). *Vital Speeches of the Day* 401–404.

Ruggiero, Vincent Ryan (1987, August 15). *Vital Speeches of the Day* 671–672.

Silber, John R. (1985, September 15). *Vital Speeches of the Day* 51.

Simonson, Brenda W. (1986, July 1). *Vital Speeches of the Day* 52.

Snyder, Richard (1984, January 1). *Vital Speeches of the Day* 51.

Sprague, Jo and Douglas Stuart (1992). *The Speaker's Handbook,* 3rd ed. San Diego: Harcourt Brace Jovanovich.

Stark, Peter B. (1985, October 1). *Vital Speeches of the Day.*

Tankersley, G. J. (1984, December 1). *Vital Speeches of the Day* 51.

Weaver, Richard L. (1991, August 1). *Vital Speeches of the Day* 620–623.